Trees, maps, and theorems

Effective communication for rational minds

Jean-luc Doumont

Principiæ
Structuring thoughts

Kraainem, Belgium
www.principiae.be

To Colin and Layla

for everything they taught me
on effective communication

About this book

I N QUEST OF SOLID WRITTEN SUPPORT for the participants of my training sessions, I searched libraries, bookstores, and mail-order catalogs, but to no avail: I did not find a reference that quite matched the approach I had developed. Encouraged by the feedback on my lectures and publications, I thus set to create my own book on effective communication, for my usual audiences of engineers, scientists, and managers. The outcome of this endeavor is the book you are now reading.

This book is about first principles. It is about strategy and, especially, about structure. To borrow Hemingway's words, it is about architecture, not interior decoration. It is about constructing communication deliberately and methodically. It is about reaching a given purpose with a given audience, in virtually any professional situation—and in any language.

This book is for professionals who want to master the basics, that is, to understand them clearly and apply them carefully when communicating on the job. It is for those who believe that effective communication skills are an invaluable, lifelong personal asset and who want to keep strengthening this asset. As such, it benefits students, too, notably graduate students.

This book, however, is no self-study course—no book can be. Sharpening one's skills requires practice on one's own material. Moreover, it requires feedback, for practice without feedback is of little use. Global feedback may come out of the situation (*Did I get my message across?*). A careful analysis, in contrast, requires an instructor or mentor—a human being, not a book.

This book has been described both as a minimalist user guide, with its concise instructions, carefully selected applications, and answers to frequently asked questions, and, interestingly, as a children's book, with its precise yet straightforward tone, its exposition of one topic per double page (most of the time), and its illustrations. These two descriptions are fine with me.

On what do you base your recommendations?

The guidelines in this book are based mostly on common sense and experience. They have been put to the test, not only in my own practice, but also by thousands of engineers, scientists, managers, and other professionals worldwide who took part in some of my training sessions. I hope the guidelines can be as useful to you as they apparently are to these professionals.

Moreover, my approach is no doubt influenced by my education as an engineer and scientist, and—in ways difficult to trace or to quantify— by all I have read or heard on communication.

Do you rely on empirical research at all?

Well-conducted research in any scholarly field is normally thought-provoking at the very least, so research findings should not be disregarded. Still, empirical research about communication suffers from very many confounding factors and is thus hard to generalize toward practice. In my experience, far too many people apply poorly understood research outcomes blindly, sometimes to the extent of generating myths. I would rather that they thought for themselves.

Why such a focus on counterexamples?

Remarkably, there is nothing quite remarkable about instances of effective communication: they draw one's attention to the ideas expressed, not to themselves, so they are hard to learn from by imitation without the contrasting viewpoint provided by a counterexample. Also, learning to pinpoint shortcomings in one's own practice is a necessary step toward improving on them.

How to use this book

This book was designed to propose a logical flow for the discussion while enabling selective reading of individual parts, chapters, or sections. Feel free, therefore, to read the complete discussion linearly or to jump ahead to the themes of interest to you. Topics are discussed in one double page each time (or in a small integer number of them), to facilitate their direct access or out-of-sequence processing.

The pages, too, are formatted for selective reading. The right page is reserved for the main discussion, with illustrations, limited examples, or comments placed left of the text. In relation to this discussion, the left page answers frequently asked questions collected at the occasion of lectures and workshops, set on a gray background. In the remaining space, it lists typical shortcomings, offers practical advice on specific subtopics, or broadens the discussion.

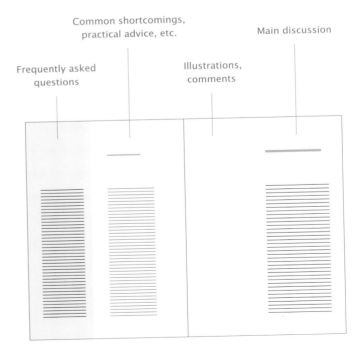

Common shortcomings, practical advice, etc.

Main discussion

Frequently asked questions

Illustrations, comments

This book is organized in five parts: first, fundamentals, then written documents, oral presentations, and graphical displays, and finally application to five more specific types of document. It ends with notes and references, as well as an index of topics.

Part one, *Fundamentals*, introduces the ideas that underpin the four subsequent parts. Probably the most arduous part of the book as it lacks the examples that appear further on, it can be skimmed or perhaps skipped at first by the reader eager to start work on documents, presentations, or displays. Still, it answers many a *why* about further recommendations and, by offering a minimal set of universal principles, it equips readers for most challenges of professional communication.

Part two, *Effective written documents*, offers a methodology in five steps to proceed from scratch to a complete document, namely planning, designing, drafting, formatting, and revising the document to be created. It details each of these five steps.

Part three, *Effective oral presentations*, proposes a similar yet distinct approach in five steps: planning the presentation, designing it, creating slides (if any), delivering the presentation, and answering questions. Though meant to stand on its own, it does not repeat uselessly what has already been discussed in detail about written documents, in particular planning.

Part four, *Effective graphical displays*, first classifies pictures as a way to help readers choose the right representation, then discusses how to plan, design, and construct optimal graphs, and finally how to draft a caption that gets the message across.

Part five, *Applications*, illustrates how the general guidelines in the previous parts apply to five common types of documents. Specifically, it examines sets of instructions, electronic mail, Web sites, meeting reports, and scientific posters, each time particularizing earlier recommendations or adding new ones.

My thanks to...

Geneviève Casterman

for her unfailing loving support
and her shrewd business advice.

Annick Vandercammen

for her review of the manuscript
and her sharp eye for consistency.

Philippe Vandenbroeck

with whom I refined my thoughts
about "choosing the right graph."

David Lougee

for a first chance to help others
sharpen their presentation skills.

... and many more people

who have attended my lectures
or workshops, have put my ideas
and recommendations to the test,
have given me valuable insights,
and have made my job rewarding.

Contents

*There is nothing so practical
as a good theory.*

— Kurt Lewin

*Ajoutez quelquefois
et souvent effacez.*

— Nicolas Boileau

Fundamentals

ALL FORMS OF EFFECTIVE COMMUNICATION—written, oral, or graphical—build on the same principles, addressing fundamental concerns of purpose, content, and form. What are we trying to achieve by engaging in communication? What must we then write, say, or draw, and how must we write, say, or draw it to reach our purpose? These are the key questions to analyze existing documents, presentations, or displays, and to create effective new ones.

This first part discusses the fundamentals of communication. After establishing what *effective communication* designates, it proposes a set of three laws that forms the very foundation of the further guidelines. As a more substantial dichotomy than the usual opposition between oral and written channels, it discusses the specificities of verbal and nonverbal codings. Finally, it examines the effectiveness of essential structures in terms of the number, hierarchy, and sequence of elements.

The name of the game

Information

*A concentration of 175 µg per m³
has been observed in urban areas*

A message

*The concentration in urban areas
(175 µg/m³) is unacceptably high*

A *what* caption (a noun phrase)
Evolution of sales over the years

A *so what* caption (a statement)
Sales dropped by 40% last year

Get your audience to

■ pay attention to,
■ understand,
■ (be able to) act upon

a maximum of messages,
given constraints.

EFFECTIVE COMMUNICATION is getting messages across. Thus it implies someone else: it is about an audience, and it suggests that we get this audience to understand something. To ensure that they understand it, we must first get them to pay attention. In turn, getting them to understand is usually nothing but a means to an end: we may want them to remember the material communicated, be convinced of it, or, ultimately, act or at least be able to act on the basis of it.

A message differs from raw information in that it presents "intelligent added value", that is, something to understand about the information. A message interprets the information for a specific audience and for a specific purpose. It conveys the *so what*, whereas information merely conveys the *what*. A message is to information what conclusions are to findings. Because it makes a statement, it requires a complete sentence.

To communicate effectively, we must thus identify messages. Conveying information only is usually not enough, as it leaves the audience with the question, so what? We must moreover recognize and seize opportunities to get the messages across, for example in the captions of figures or in the titles of slides.

Often, the messages to be conveyed are numerous or complex, and the situation carries constraints. Among these are space (such as a four-page limit on a paper), time (a 15-minute limit on a presentation), and audience (background, language, etc.). Not every hindrance is a true constraint, though: for example, a suboptimal room can often be rearranged, at least to a point.

Effective communication is optimization under constraints: we must maximize, not what we write, say, or draw, but how much our audience gets out of our documents, presentations, and displays, in quantity or in quality—with a purpose in mind and under certain constraints. Because of these constraints, we cannot hope to be perfect. We can, however, be optimal.

The three laws of communication

THREE SIMPLE YET SOLID PRINCIPLES are all we need to optimize virtually any instance of communication. These three "laws of communication" can be derived with a simple model of one-way communication, embodying the idea of getting messages across optimally to our audience.

First law   Adapt to your audience

To optimize under constraints, we must first identify what is and what is not under our control, and concentrate on what is. To a point, we cannot select our audience: we must take them as they come. Still, we can decide what to tell them and how. To optimize our communication, we must thus adapt to them.

Second law   Maximize the signal-to-noise ratio

The simple model above is ideal: it suggests that information or messages sent from one side reach the other side intact. In practice, information may suffer losses, because of noise. To prevent losses, we must filter out the noise; alternatively, we can enhance the signal so it can withstand the noise better.

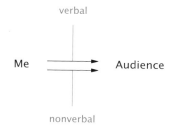

Third law   Use effective redundancy

The second law is limited to prevention. When noise cannot be anticipated, it cannot be filtered out, so it results in losses. To compensate for the losses, we can tell things several times, by repeating the message or by replicating it across channels, preferably in different ways, such as verbally and nonverbally.

Real-world audiences know less

Can I not select my audience at all?

Early on, the audience is not necessarily given, indeed: a scientist deciding to which journal to send a paper is selecting his or her audience. Still, the range of options is often limited and, once a journal has been chosen, the audience becomes a given: the scientist can hardly select, within this audience, who may read the paper.

Can I not change or influence my audience?

You can most certainly influence your audience, such as increase their motivation or provide any prerequisite knowledge they might need. In doing so, you are already communicating with them and, essentially, adapting to them. In other words, the audience can be regarded as given in that they cannot be changed a priori. Influencing them requires adapting to them.

Why should I always be the one adapting?

You should be the one adapting to the extent that you are the one with a purpose—that is, that you want something from your audience. Much like being customer-minded in business or being user-friendly in software development, adapting to one's audience is really a question of effectiveness more than one of selflessness.

Is the audience never to be blamed, then?

Blaming the audience may help us feel better but seldom gets us anywhere, unless perhaps if blames can influence the audience positively. A more purpose-oriented approach is to regard their shortcomings as constraints—and adapt.

Adapting to the audience in a professional context is all the more difficult because practice in school usually develops the wrong communication reflexes. Real-world audiences and purposes differ markedly from those that students were long confronted with.

Students formally write and speak to demonstrate their mastery of a well-defined body of knowledge and, ultimately, to be graded. For such a purpose, their only relevant audience is the course instructor: a single, clearly identified person, who is normally more knowledgeable than they are about the topic and morally obliged to read their entire document or attend their entire presentation, however boring. Accordingly, successful strategies to good grades may involve including as much material as possible (especially when in doubt as to what the instructor will give extra credit for) or showing off with jargon.

Professionals, in contrast, formally write and speak to get their audiences to pay attention, understand, and (be able to) act. Such real-world audiences are unpredictably multiple (especially for documents), almost always less knowledgeable about the topic, and highly selective about what they read or attend. They have little patience with writers and, especially, speakers attempting to demonstrate the breadth or depth of their knowledge, often at the expense of the clarity or the conciseness of their discourse.

Unsurprisingly, the most common failure to adapt to one's audience, then, is to present information that is too technical or too little relevant to them. According to a common myth in academic research, a presentation should have one third that everyone in the audience understands, one third that some understand, and one third that no one understands. What can one gain with such an approach, though? Audiences have infinitely more respect for speakers who can explain complex matters in simple ways and thus give new insights. Still, the myth endures.

Adapting to the audience

EFFECTIVE COMMUNICATION always requires motivation. If we want our audience to pay attention to, understand, and act upon our messages, we are the ones who should make the effort. That is, we must adapt to them, not expect them to adapt to us. Should they be willing and able to adapt, too, so much the better, but we have no cause to assume they will.

The first law, *adapt to your audience*, is one of empowerment: it implies that we are responsible for the success of our acts of communication. If our audiences fail to get the messages, it is our problem, not theirs, as we have not reached our goal. Blaming them makes little sense: it hardly helps us optimize. From our perspective, the degrees of freedom are on our side.

Adapting to our audience is normally a spontaneous attitude in our private life. For example, we do not address children the way we address adults: we recognize the need to adapt. It is far less spontaneous an attitude in our professional life, in which we tend to regard the others as similar to ourselves.

Adapting means putting ourselves in the shoes of the audience, anticipating their situation, their needs, their expectations, etc. It implies structuring the story along their line of reasoning, not ours, and recognizing the constraints they might bring: their familiarity with the topic, their mastery of the language, the time they can free for us, etc. Whenever we are not taking a certain constraint into account somehow, we fail to adapt.

Finally, adapting to the audience suggests that, if one strategy does not work, we try a different one. If the audience failed to get the message, merely repeating it is unlikely to help: we must change the code or the channel. As the saying goes, if we do what we already did, we will get what we already got. Still, adapting to our audience does not mean losing track of our purpose. On the contrary, it means doing what it takes to get the audience to (be able to) do what we want them to do.

Teachers who stick to what they had planned to do regardless of whether the students pay attention, understand, or develop the required competencies are not adapting to their audience. Unsurprisingly, such teachers often blame it all on the students, too.

Imagine that a foreigner asks you for directions and that the only language you have in common with him is English, of which he has little command. Suppose that he did not get your first explanation. Adapting to him (assuming that you are motivated) might involve making gestures, sketching a map, speaking more slowly, pronouncing more clearly, using a simpler vocabulary and a simpler syntax— or perhaps accompanying him to where he must go.

Identifying sources of noise

*Is noise always bad? Can it not be used
to regain the attention of the audience?*

Noise is undesirable by definition. If something
helps you reach the purpose you have in mind,
such as by getting the attention of the audience,
you can best regard it as signal, not as noise.

Still, before introducing or tolerating anything
that might attract attention, consider whether
the device does not distract more than it helps,
such as by stealing the attention away from you
or reflecting badly on your professional image.
When they are handled with a touch of humor,
minor mishaps in an oral presentation can help
the speaker build rapport with the audience,
yet the presentation would be more impressive
without them. Similarly, conspicuous clothes
or jewelry can easily overshadow the message.
Attendees later referring to one of the speakers
as *you know, the one with the dark red jacket*
remember the clothes more than the person.

*How can I "increase the signal"
beyond merely speaking louder?*

Increasing the volume in an oral presentation
or perhaps the font size in a written document
seem obvious applications of the second law,
as is making the data lines thicker than the axes,
tick marks, or grid lines in a graphical display.

More broadly, *increasing the signal* may mean
conveying stronger messages. When we do not
master the language, when the transmission is
unusually poor, or when the audience is tired
or otherwise less attentive, we may well have
to be blunt and not attempt to be too subtle,
as subtleties will probably not survive the noise.
While not ideal, it would be optimal in this case.

Noise comes in many forms and from many sources.
In the case of a formal presentation, for example,
the noise sources that most people readily think of
are the audience and the environment: attendees
chatting among themselves or coming in and out,
mobile phones going off, noisy air conditioning,
unreliable equipment (microphone, projector, etc.),
building works in progress outside the room, etc.
The noise source that these people forget at first
is the speaker himself or herself. Noise produced
by a speaker is typically more distracting than that
coming from other sources, because it is part of
what the audience is supposed to pay attention to.
Just because it comes from the speaker, however,
it can more easily be controlled than other sources.

Noise produced by speakers in oral presentations
shows more particularly in two components: slides
and delivery. Busy slides compete with the speaker
for the attention of the audience, and flashy slides
draw attention to themselves, not to their content.
Delivery noise includes imperfect pronunciation,
filler words, unnecessary gestures or mannerisms,
and so on, all the way to inappropriate dress code.

Noise in documents is whatever prompts readers
to stop thinking about content and start thinking
about form (or perhaps about irrelevant content).
Examples are an unclear structure of the document,
intricate sentences, unusual or superfluous words,
spelling mistakes, and distracting visual elements
in the figures, the typography, or the page layout.

Noise in graphical displays includes the many forms
of data distortion, as with inappropriate graph types,
and all "unnecessary ink", that is, visual elements
that can be erased without loss of clarity or accuracy:
decorative third dimensions or gradients of color
and overabundant tick marks or grid lines in graphs,
irrelevant backgrounds or objects in photographs
(to be removed ahead of time or cropped out), etc.

Maximizing the signal-to-noise ratio

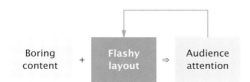

A frequent yet hopeless attempt: salvaging uninteresting content with an "interesting" page layout. Will the document thus produced get the attention of the audience? Yes, it will—on the page layout, with little transfer to the content, if any. The flashy layout is noise.

NOTHING IS NEUTRAL in communication. The audience indeed sees and hears everything, so everything matters. What does not help get the message across detracts from it by needlessly mobilizing the audience's intellectual resources, even if for a short time. By definition, it is noise. Noise is thus more than unwanted sound: it is anything that can distract from the message (the signal) by drawing attention onto itself.

Noise can be a major impediment to effective communication. At best, it just stretches the attention span of the audience. At worst, it takes their attention entirely away from the content. As an example, typographical errors in a written document or filler words in an oral presentation can be most distracting: audience members may well find themselves on the lookout for the next typo or next *um* rather than for the next message. In graphical communication, noise easily shifts the attention from content to technology: when readers start wondering what software produced a graph instead of what experiment produced the data, they are most probably missing the point.

The second law, *maximize the signal-to-noise ratio* (or *ratios*), is all about contrast between what helps and what hinders an act of communication. The ratio between signal and noise matters more than signal or noise alone. To a point, we can thus tolerate continuous background noise, which we notice only when it varies suddenly, for example when it goes away.

Clearly, the most satisfying approach to contrast is reducing or eliminating noise: breaking the silence in a whisper is far more effective than covering the noise in a shout. Recognizing that nothing is neutral, we should thus question the relevance of anything we plan to include: words in a written document, gestures in an oral presentation, lines in a graphical display. To optimize a text or an image, we may do better to suppress, not add. By removing every unneeded drop of ink, we ensure that the audience pays attention to nothing but the message.

Identifying possible codings

Is redundancy the same as repetition?

Repetition suggests a signal at different times on one channel, as when a speaker previews his or her main points before developing them. Redundancy can be just that, but it can also be a signal across different channels at one time, as when a speaker illustrates the presentation with a slide show. Either way can be effective.

Why insist on calling it "effective" redundancy?

Not all redundancy is effective. For example, superfluous words as in *added bonus* or *oval in shape* add nothing. What is much worse still, multiple channels competing with one another, such as text-heavy slides accompanying a talk, are more harmful than helpful: each channel is indeed a source of noise for the other one(s).

Is a channel the same as a coding?

The term *channel* (or, equivalently, *medium*) refers to perception by the senses; in contrast, *coding* refers more to processing by the mind. (At times, the boundary is somewhat blurred.) For example, *paper* conveying written words or *air* conveying oral words (as sound waves) are channels, and *text* or *pictures* are codings.

What matters most for effective redundancy is codings. In first approximation, text is text, whether it is seen through the eyes or heard through the ears. A different coding, such as a picture, would be a more useful redundancy than a similar coding in a different channel, such as a second stream of text. Still, channels have their importance, in particular in terms of the nature of the noise they are subject to.

The three laws are in order of decreasing priority. To prevent losses, the first measure is to filter out the noise and, if deemed useful, increase the signal (adapting its maximum intensity to the audience). If we could filter out all noise, we would not need redundancy, at least not to compensate for losses, because there would not be any. Alas, some noise is beyond our control: attendees at a presentation may be preoccupied with something else, readers of a document may be interrupted by a phone call, etc. Using several codings is thus usually desirable.

Because nothing is neutral, most everything can be regarded as a coding, that is, as a potential source of noise if left uncontrolled and a potential signal if used well. Whether or not we like it, the clothes we wear always say something about who we are, for example. While we may decide not to worry unduly about the possible statement we thus make because it has far less impact than other codings, we may want to scrutinize our dress code for noise.

Devices we can usefully regard as distinct codings in written documents include the text itself, the set of headings in the text and in the table of contents, the page layout (revealing the structure visually), and tables or figures, all of which can be optimized.

In oral presentations, codings include most of all the verbal, vocal, and visual delivery (all three being powerful devices toward convincing an audience), possibly supported by slides or printed handouts. Just because the nonverbal ones (vocal and visual) are intuitive does not mean they cannot be managed: we can thus learn to amplify our intonation, quiet body noise, or make eye contact with the audience.

Graphical displays, too, can be seen as including more than one coding. They might convey meaning through relative lengths, positions along a scale, shapes, colors, explanatory labels, captions, etc.

Using effective redundancy

The stop sign conveys meaning through shape, color, and label: it is the only octagonal sign, one of only two signs to be solid red (the other is the wrong-way sign), and the only one labeled "STOP" in most countries. It also comes with a white line across the lane as yet another way to mean stop.

Telling things once is often not enough: redundancy helps restore messages damaged by noise. It should not, however, introduce noise itself, that is, distract the audience, such as when concurrent channels compete with one another. Effective redundancy, therefore, gets a given message across several times, but coded in complementary, compatible ways.

Effective redundancy works in two ways: one is compensation, the other, collaboration. First, each coding gives the audience a chance to understand the message. Motorists, for example, can identify a stop sign in three ways: color, label, and shape. If they cannot distinguish the color, they can read the label "STOP." If this label is hidden by mud or snow (or if they see the sign from the back), they can still recognize it by shape. By giving several chances, effective redundancy helps address inhomogeneous audiences. Second, all codings work together in synergy: here, color, label, and shape, when all identified, complement one another for a faster recognition of the sign.

What makes a different coding is partly a view of the mind. Though they are both verbal codings on the same medium, the text and the headings within a document can be regarded as distinct codings, used for distinct purposes. When looking for a specific part of the document, we are thus likely to flip through the pages and look at the headings but not at the text. Conversely, when we have decided to read the full document linearly, we typically read the text but skip all the headings.

Although redundancy is a choice, the multiplicity of codings may not be: some codings are unavoidable. When speaking in public, for example, we communicate through what we say (the verbal component), how we say it (the vocal component), and everything that we let the audience see about ourselves (the visual component). Any component escaping our control can carry noise or, what is worse, convey messages that work against our intent, resulting in so-called cognitive dissonance.

Fundamentals

The name of the game
The three laws of communication
A thousand words, a thousand pictures
Chains and magical numbers
Trees, maps, and theorems

Effective written documents

Planning the document
Designing the document
Drafting the document
Formatting the document
Revising the document

Effective oral presentations

Planning the presentation
Designing the presentation
Creating slides
Delivering the presentation
Answering questions

Effective graphical displays

Understanding pictures
Planning the graph
Designing the graph
Constructing the graph
Drafting the caption

Applications

Effective instructions
Effective electronic mail
Effective Web sites
Effective meeting reports
Effective scientific posters

A thousand words, a thousand pictures

Verbal	**Nonverbal**
text-like	vocal, visual
Rational	**Intuitive**
abstract, learned	concrete, innate
Sequential	**Global**
slow, exclusive	fast, nonexclusive

A PICTURE IS WORTH A THOUSAND WORDS, or so they say. In reality, however, not all pictures are created equal, and the power of visual communication is too often misunderstood, not to say misused. Pictures are no panacea; some words convey concepts better than a thousand pictures.

Intellectual processes, complex and still poorly understood, can pragmatically be modeled as either verbal or nonverbal. Verbal processes are rational, able to manipulate intangible, abstract concepts whose symbolic meaning must be learned. Nonverbal processes are intuitive, almost unconscious, tuned for concrete items with nonsymbolic, quasi innate meaning. Verbal code, such as a piece of text, is sequential; as a result, it is processed relatively slowly. In contrast, nonverbal code, such as a photograph, is global and processed in an instant. Verbal and nonverbal processes are about codes, not channels: as an example, text is verbal code, whether it is heard or read.

Verbal and nonverbal processes are independent of each other so they can take place concurrently: for example, an audience can watch a static picture while listening to an explanation. Concurrent verbal processes, however, are mutually exclusive: for example, an audience cannot both read text on the screen and listen to spoken text, unless perhaps if it is the same text.

Nonverbal codings, being intuitive, usually have more impact than verbal ones. To some extent, they are also more credible: we believe tone of voice and body language more than words. Dissonance between verbal and nonverbal codings can be put to good use in irony and in humor, when we let our audience know nonverbally that we do not mean what we say verbally, but is otherwise dangerous. Thus a pictorial representation of what *not* to do is misleading, even when it is accompanied by a text explanation, unless the *not* is expressed visually, too. Likewise, graphs can be intentionally or accidentally deceptive, and no amount of text can fully correct the visual deception.

Although the left scale tells us (rationally) that the difference between 1999 and 2000 is 1.5%, the visual code prevails: we keep from the graph a strong, lasting feeling that the value for 2000 was twice that for 1999.

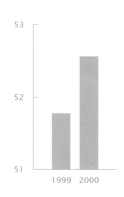

Removing visual noise

Why are nonverbal codings more credible?

Body language is typically more spontaneous than words are: nonverbal codings are harder to control, hence less likely to be manipulated (the body never lies, according to the proverb). As audience members, we might reason thus and decide to believe the body. More probably, however, we do not reason about the conflict: we absorb nonverbal codings unconsciously, without the analytical filter we apply to words. In other words, we believe nonverbal codings because we have no process to disbelieve them. We instantly sense that the words are untrue.

Can I never include text on presentation slides?

If your oral presentation must discuss a text, for example a novel or an article from a treaty, you might be justified in including some of it on your slides: this text is your very material and no longer a mere support for it. If you do, limit the text excerpts to those strictly needed to make your points. When showing the slide, read the text excerpt out loud for the audience, so they can read it together with you, then have their mental text processor available to handle what you have to tell them about the excerpt.

Text, here, implies sequential processing, as in a sequence of words whose order is dictated by syntax, or perhaps a sequence of sentences. Words that do not form a text and can thus be read in any order, as the labels on a diagram, are less of an issue on slides, since they do not conflict as much with concurrent spoken text. Conversely, animated visual representations, while not textual, are processed sequentially: it may be hard to watch an animated diagram and follow spoken discourse at the same time.

Pictures are powerful, and what is powerful is risky. In a verbal coding, and possible connotations aside, the conventional meaning is all that really matters: the word *apple* means "apple"—no more, no less. In contrast, in a visual coding, everything matters: the minutiae of the shape, the shades of color, etc. If such details help get a relevant message across, they are welcome indeed; otherwise, they are noise. Pictures, in other words, carry a higher potential for noise than text. It is usually easier to choose the right word than to come up with the right picture.

When details are irrelevant or otherwise undesirable, as is usually the case in technical communication, photographs can best be replaced by sober line art, less likely to carry irrelevant details. A human hand in a realistic illustration, for example of someone inserting an extension card in an electronic device, is not just any hand: it has a color, gender, and age, not to mention social status and grooming habits. A more schematic representation (line art) displays a hand with which more viewers are able to identify.

Even the most sober line art has its limits, however. The mind is so prompt to recognize visual patterns that it often interprets images in unintended ways. For example, it is as good as impossible to draw a person—or even an animal—without conveying an attitude, which may or may not be well received. Such an attitude, so conspicuous in most clip art, is noticeable even in silhouettes and in stick figures.

14

A picture excels at representing something intuitive, for example a real object. At the same time, it is condemned to be concrete: it cannot convey abstract ideas (at any rate not unambiguously).

As an example of the ubiquitous visual ambiguity, the attitude of this little boy is read differently by different people: is he serene, sad, interested, absentminded? What do *you* see in this picture?

Visual codings, being intuitive and global, are more effective for conveying intuitive or global information. For example, maps convey relative positions more rapidly than words can, drawings describe objects more clearly than words can, and facial expressions show emotions more subtly than words can. Visual codings that mimic facial expressions such as ";-)" have thus emerged in such plain-text media as electronic mail, to convey meaning that relies on intuition—typically humor.

Visual codings, by contrast, are less effective for expressing abstract concepts. A given pictorial representation illustrates only one instance of a concept so easily expressed in words. As an example, a photograph of an apple does not say "apple": rather, it indicates a specimen of specific variety, maturity, etc. as suggested by the apple's visible shape, texture, and color. Nonsymbolic representations are condemned to be concrete, even if schematic drawings can "abstract" irrelevant details, thus broadening the drawing's suggested meaning somewhat.

Visual codings, moreover, lack the accuracy that words are endowed with through conventional association of meaning. Just like Rorschach inkblots, they are intrinsically ambiguous: being intuitive and concrete, they suggest a meaning instantly and may well suggest a different meaning to each viewer, often unable to imagine anyone else "seeing" anything else.

In a sense, a word is worth a thousand pictures, too. Indeed, verbal codings can express abstract concepts unambiguously and concisely, even if not intuitively. As an example, the word *apple* designates any apple and thus transcends all pictures, which can show specimens only. Words can convey concepts that nonsymbolic codings cannot, for example interdiction: showing it visually requires a convention, such as a red circle.

In essence, verbal and nonverbal codings are complementary. They are perhaps the essential form of effective redundancy.

Chains and magical numbers

A sequence   A hierarchy

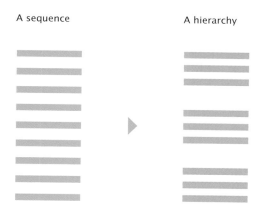

OUR CAPACITY FOR PROCESSING unstructured items of information presented together is severely limited. Series of items, or lists, tax our short-term memory, key to mental processing, and become rapidly unmanageable as the number of items grows beyond just a few. *Processing* and *short-term memory* suggest random access to the items. Longer lists can of course be committed to long-term memory by rote learning, but this memory provides sequential access only: if we forget one link in the chain, we often cannot go on. As a rule, we can process items in random fashion if we can see at a glance how many there are, without having to count.

An *item* is whatever we can, to a point, recognize and process as a unit. To make a long list easier to process, we can group items into fewer, higher-level items, thus creating a hierarchy (a list of lists): a series of three series of three items is easier for a human brain to process than a single series of nine items. For the higher-level items to be recognized as units, however, the original items must be grouped logically, not arbitrarily. This logic must be made explicit or be readily recognizable for the audience. Visual clustering helps show the groups, too.

Balanced, multidimensional structures, in other words, match our mental patterns better than longer, unidimensional ones. Chains, structured along a single dimension, must be accessed in sequence. Trees, structured hierarchically, add a dimension. They offer, not a sequence of items, but a sequence of choices, in the form of recursive branching. They can thus organize a large number of items while offering few enough options in every choice to enable random processing of these items. With the cascade of choices kept short enough, they provide an overview of the collection of items in a way chains cannot. They are thus easier to apprehend, navigate, and remember, and constitute a more robust framework, for example to build a case: whereas a chain is only as strong as its weakest link, a weak argument in a tree does not invalidate the other ones.

How about numbering the items, so readers can "see at a glance how many there are"?

"Seeing at a glance how many items there are" is a reliable sign of nonsequential perception. This perception is about *seeing* all the items; *being told* how many there are does not help.

Is sequential processing necessarily a problem?

Admittedly, linear material—for example a set of step-by-step instructions—may at first seem to require no more than sequential processing. Still, a hierarchical structure would give users an overview of the steps to be performed, thus preparing them mentally for the tasks ahead. Moreover, a long list often intimidates readers. Tree structures typically look more accessible.

Is text not processed sequentially anyway?

A verbal list, even short, must indeed be read sequentially: word after word, item after item. *Nonsequential* here refers to the initial (visual) perception of the list of items and, especially, to their manipulation in short-term memory, where they can be, in a sense, "seen" together, reviewed in any order, and finally passed on to long-term memory in a structured manner.

Must presentations always have three points?

Presentations need not have three main points: some topics are better structured in two, four, or perhaps five points. Still, because a structure in three points communicates particularly well, you might want to give it a try systematically, without forcing it on your topic if it does not fit.

While they are harder to process, chains are easier to create than trees, because they need local effort only: they can be constructed one item at a time, with little or no attention to the structure as a whole. As the examples below illustrate, chain structures are frequent in verbal code (written or spoken text) and in nonverbal items (slide shows, graphs, etc.) alike, each time taxing the intellectual capabilities of the audience—and, in one case, of the speaker.

Long series of short sentences—perhaps written in the simplistic belief that shorter sentences are easier to read—make for hard-to-read paragraphs, even if each sentence individually is very readable. The same holds for long series of short paragraphs.

Chains of premodifiers need not be long to create uncertainty as to which words are being modified. They are often found on restaurant menus (*Grilled Applewood Smoked Bacon Wrapped Mission Figs*) and in scientific publications (*Fuzzy-Logic-Controller-Based Cost-Effective Four-Switch Three-Phase Inverter-Fed IPM Synchronous Motor Drive System*).

Writing down and committing to memory the text of a presentation places the speaker at the mercy of the slightest memory lapse: the rest of the text usually cannot be recalled past any missing words (and a gap in the text would be noticeable anyway).

Showing many slides as part of an oral presentation easily creates a disorienting impression of linearity, especially if all slides have the same visual design, that is, unless there are contrasting slides meant to reveal the hierarchical structure of the material.

Graphical displays such as pie charts that include too many items not only face the spatial challenge of labeling all segments clearly but also fail to give an overview of the data. As an alternative, bar charts can display hierarchical groups of data more easily.

The question, of course, is how long a list can reasonably be, that is, how many items presented together are too many. Rather than blindly apply a single, dogmatic "magical number," let us see how small integers can usefully guide our practice of communication. As it happens, there is magic everywhere.

Zero is perfection, as in zero superfluous words on a page, zero useless gestures in a talk, zero unneeded ink in a graph. Aiming for zero noise means much hard work for something the audience will *not* notice—frustrating, yes, but effective.

One is focus, as in one theme per document or presentation, one message per paragraph or slide, one idea per sentence. One is consistency and univocality, a prerequisite to meaning in verbal codings: synonyms and homonyms are suboptimal.

Two is a bit, a binary alternative. It is thus the simplest form of classification, as in specialist versus nonspecialist or verbal versus nonverbal. Two is a duality, with all its appeal and all its limitation, as in good and evil, night and day, yin and yang. Besides opposition or complementarity, two is redundancy across channels or codings—a potentially effective approach.

Three is the simplest complexity: it corresponds to a triangle (the first polygon), the number of dimensions in physical space, and the number of colors required to generate all the others. Three is of course a direct extension of two, one that breaks the duality, as by introducing gray between black and white. Interestingly, three is how we group digits in large numbers for increased readability. It is a common-sense upper limit in many cases, for example on the number of heading levels that can meaningfully be numbered together (*Section 2.4.1*). Pragmatically, three is probably the optimal number for items that must be grasped rapidly and remembered easily, such as steps in a procedure or main points in an oral presentation. Three items simply work well—for speaker and audience alike.

I thought seven was "the" magical number and a universal upper limit. Is it not so?

George Miller's now famous article published in 1956 in *Psychological Review*, "The magical number seven, plus or minus two: Some limits on our capacity for processing information," is frequently misunderstood and misquoted. It derives seven as a rough asymptotical limit from experiments that are in fact little relevant to the type of communication discussed here. Anyway, to reduce the risk of processing errors, we should limit the number of items presented together to fewer than the asymptotical value. Pragmatically, we could use the lower bound of Miller's proposed 7 ± 2 interval, namely five.

How can I group items in a table that is not otherwise structured?

You can always group the rows visually by five (or fewer), as by skipping space every five rows or, when space is at a premium, by alternating the background color for groups of five rows. Though not dictated by logic, such a grouping makes the rows of the table easier to read off, especially when the columns are set far apart.

Should rating scales not have some kind of neutral between positive and negative?

The middle point provided by an odd number of options may be desirable, but it can become an easy noncommittal retreat (though perhaps mitigated by an out-of-scale *no opinion* option). Still, three options (+/o/−) provide no degree of positive or negative appreciation, while five are already enough to drive some respondents into avoiding the two extremes systematically.

The difficulty is combinatorial

The abrupt saturation, beyond five, of our capacity for processing a set of items presented together may come as a surprise. Going from five to six items means adding only 20% to the sequence, whereas going from two to three is adding 50%—a lot more. We might thus expect processing six items instead of five to be 2.5 times easier than processing three instead of two, yet experience suggests otherwise.

One plausible explanation is combinatorial analysis. Because the key to apprehending sequences fully is the possibility to process them nonsequentially, we should reason, not in terms of sequence length, but in terms of nonsequential combinations. A set of n items can be combined in $n!$ (factorial n) ways, a function that grows much more sharply than n. Going from two to three items means multiplying the possibilities by three (from $2! = 2$ to $3! = 6$); going from five to six items, by contrast, means multiplying them by six (from $5! = 120$ to $6! = 720$). This model would explain not only why six items are so much harder to handle than five but also why key items benefit from being fewer than five (three items being thus 20 times less demanding).

The sequential process required beyond five items applies to visual codes, too, as soon as their details have to be processed one by one. As an example, how easily can you identify below the differences between upper and lower drawing, besides rotation? First global, the comparison becomes sequential as the number of items increases, unless (part of) the figure becomes meaningful to you as a whole.

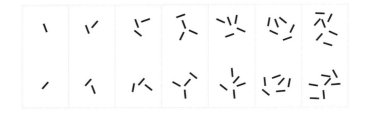

Four is a square (2^2): it is a combination of two binary options. Four is therefore a useful number of answers for rating scales ($++/+/-/--$), as it embodies a cascade of two binary choices: first, is it rather positive or negative; next, is it a little or a lot. Four is also a direct extension of three: whatever works well in threes might also work, though not nearly as well, in fours. While large numbers are usually set in groups of three digits, a year such as 1984 is set as a single group of all four digits, with no apparent readability problem (yet it is read in English as *nineteen eighty-four*, or 2×2 digits). As another example, whereas *Section 2.4.1* is reasonably easy to situate mentally or to remember, *Section 2.4.1.3* is immediately much harder.

Five is a handful: it is the number of fingers on a human hand but also the limit above which we must count items to know their number—unless they are organized visually in groups of five or less, as can usefully be done with rows in long tables. It is thus a useful upper limit on the number of items in a list.

Six is… just after five, the same way that four is just after three. Consequently, if five is a useful maximum number for a group of items not otherwise structured, then six is just past the limit. In other words, six might work for some people, in some cases.

Seven is many: it is usually too many for the communication to be effective. In a sense, seven is the smallest numerousness, in the same way three is the simplest complexity: seven items presented together are just too numerous to be manageable. Apart perhaps for overwhelming the audience economically, seven is not a particularly useful number for communication.

From the eight numbers above, and beyond the obvious zero and one, you might remember the first three prime numbers: two for effective redundancy, as with verbal versus nonverbal; three as an optimal number—fast to grasp, easy to remember; five as the maximum number that ensures global processing.

Trees, maps, and theorems

STRUCTURE IS A VIEW OF THE MIND. While one scheme may well seem more logical than alternative ones, none is inexorably prescribed by the material to be presented. Organizing material involves choice, so it allows optimization. The optimal structure is the one that makes the most sense for the audience. In other words, it is easy for the audience to recognize and remember, it can be navigated effortlessly even if not memorized, and it limits the need for navigation.

Organizing knowledge effectively requires a hierarchy: a tree, not a chain. At the same time, any instance of communication is trapped in time and forms a sequence: a chain, not a tree. At an elementary level, verbal discourse is indeed sequential: words, sentences, etc., are read or heard one after the other, and their order largely determines the meaning of the text. At a higher level, even reasonably self-sufficient components such as independent chapters, slides, or graphical displays are presented in a certain sequence. In an oral presentation, this sequence is imposed by the speaker; in a document, it is proposed by the writer but ultimately chosen by each reader, who elects both what to read and in what order to read it. Still, sequence there is: even highly selective readers cannot read two different chapters of a document at the same time.

Engineering our communication, then, is a triple challenge: we must organize our material into a well-balanced hierarchy, reveal this hierarchy through what is unavoidably a sequence in time, and ensure that the sequence we propose or impose suits the logic of the audience—and all of this, at all levels, from an entire document or presentation all the way down to a single sentence, which embodies the structure of an idea. Here again, effective redundancy is sure to help. A structure already revealed by verbal discourse can be visualized ideally by nonverbal code, processed globally. The layout of pages or slides (and, especially, of the table of contents or preview) thus plays a key role in revealing a structure to the audience.

Common ineffective structures

How should I number the sections?

As a rule, use the so-called decimal numbering, as in *2.4.1* to indicate Subsection 1 of Section 4 of Chapter 2: it makes the hierarchy apparent. In contrast, selecting a single number or letter for the subsection, as in *IV* or *D*, fails to reveal its place within the overall structure: readers may not remember what it is the fourth part of, especially if they must interrupt their reading or when they are browsing through a document.

To remain readable, decimal numbering is best limited to three levels. Fourth-level headings, if any, can be set without a number. Similarly, when a book includes parts, the part number can probably be omitted from the numbering of the part's chapters, sections, and subsections.

Why a different number of levels and of items for written documents and oral presentations?

Listeners are in a far less favorable situation than readers to process the material presented: for example, they cannot choose their rhythm, cannot reread a part they did not understand, and have fewer visual clues about the structure (as offered to readers by a document's layout). They therefore cannot assimilate as complex a structure as readers can and should thus be presented, when possible, with simpler ones.

Also, presentations and documents normally differ in their purpose. Oral presentations are for convincing an audience of the key messages, while written documents more often attempt to convey a large or complex body of material. Presentations can thus typically accommodate a simpler structure, whereas (long) documents often require a somewhat more elaborate one.

Long documents (reports, theses, procedures, etc.) tend to include too many levels in their hierarchy, perhaps with few items at each level—a structure that extends in depth, often with heading numbers such as 2.3.2.1.1.2 that no longer allow readers to visualize the hierarchy. Here, "too many levels" mean more than three or just more than necessary, as when there are almost more headings than text.

At the same time, there is of course nothing wrong with deeply structured thinking. What is suboptimal is turning each item of a mental tree into a heading. Perhaps each lowest-level item in one's mental tree can be written as one paragraph or one sentence, with fewer (levels of) headings in the tree structure.

Deep structure

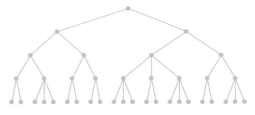

Flat structure

Shorter documents for less specialized audiences, such as magazines and newsletters, often simplify the hierarchy to an extreme, keeping only one level of heading. In the process, however, they end up with many headings at this level—a flat structure, by no means easier to assimilate than a deep one.

For a well-balanced structure, generate for yourself a complete table of contents. Are there many levels? Many headings on few pages? Single subbranches?

Balancing the structure

AN EFFECTIVE STRUCTURE IS HIERARCHICAL, not sequential. Furthermore, it consists of a limited number of levels and a limited number of items at every level. Each such item must form a meaningful entity—one comparable in scope to other entities at the same level, within and across branches. Items within a branch should be preceded by a component that gives a motivation for the branch, previews its structure implicitly or explicitly, and perhaps states its main messages. (The guidelines below apply to the levels of the tree revealed through headings and perhaps numbering, such as chapters and sections, not to levels such as paragraphs and sentences.)

As a rule, use fewer hierarchical levels than items per level, for we handle recursion with even more difficulty than lists. In written documents, endeavor to limit the number of levels to three—for example, chapters, sections, and subsections. If you must group paragraphs within a subsection, consider unnumbered headings, which would not appear in the table of contents. In oral presentations, limit yourself to one level for a short presentation, perhaps two levels for a longer one.

Limit the number of items per level, too, like you do for lists. In written documents, aim for no more than five subbranches for each branch, to afford readers a global view of the branch. Should you seem to need more, group closely related ones and substructure the entity thus obtained with paragraphs. If you have too many chapters, try grouping them into parts. In oral presentations, consider a body in exactly three points.

Before dividing a branch in subbranches, provide a global view. In written documents, include a paragraph (or more) between the heading of, say, a section and that of the first subsection. Among other things, this paragraph must let readers know what the subsections are, as a form of effective redundancy with the set of headings in the text and in the table of contents. In oral presentations, include a preview just before the body.

Well-balanced structure

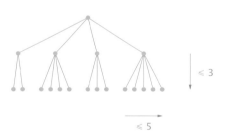

$\leqslant 3$

$\leqslant 5$

With up to three levels in the tree (chapters, sections, subsections) and up to five items at each level, a balanced document could thus have up to $5^3 = 125$ subsections, which is plenty for most material. Exceptions to this limit of 5^3 are of course possible when justified.

Navigation: more than a Web site story

What is wrong with a detailed table of contents on several pages? Does it not enable readers to locate precisely what they are looking for?

Readers may or may not know what to look for in a document (or what the document calls it). When they do, they are best helped by an index, not a table of contents, no matter how detailed. When they do not, or more generally to form an overview of the material, they will normally go through the table of contents hierarchically, not sequentially, identifying first the chapter most likely to be of interest for their purpose, then the section within this chapter, and so on. If they cannot see the whole structure at once, they have to process it sequentially; they miss an overview of the major entry point (chapters).

An alternative to limiting the number of levels presented is to provide two tables of contents: a global one, limited to the top level (chapters), then a fully detailed one. In a sense, the first is a table of contents of the table of contents.

Why must links use the wording of the map?

If links use a different wording from the map to express destinations, readers may be able to find whatever information they are seeking but not to visualize their itinerary, as the links point to places they cannot put on the map. Thus they cannot easily know when and why they might have been there before, which is a major factor in deciding whether to go there.

Using exactly the same wording on the map and in links is a simple issue of consistency: always calling a given thing by the same name helps the audience recognize this thing easily and avoids ambiguity—in links and elsewhere.

Hypertext, in a sense, predates the electronic age. While the term suggests clickable links (hyperlinks), the idea of linking a piece of text to another piece of text is not a recent one. And although new media open new possibilities, effective paper documents have provided for centuries both the motivation and the means for readers to jump to other parts of the page, to other pages, or to other documents.

Table of contents   Heading   Figure call   Index

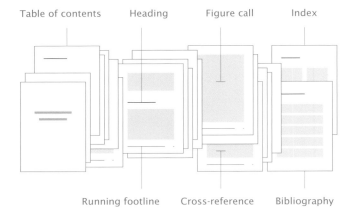

Running footline   Cross-reference   Bibliography

Effective paper documents, in particular the longer and strongly structured ones such as books, carry a surprising amount of navigational information, both by nature and by contents. As physical sets of pages, they provide clues to where readers are, such as near the beginning. Numbered headings and running headlines or footlines can further help readers locate their current position in a structure already made explicit through a table of contents. This table, perhaps together with a text overview near the end of the introduction, enables readers to make informed decisions regarding where to go. So does an index, along a different logic. Finally, the references to bibliographical entries, to tables and figures, and to other parts of the document are as many "hyperlinks"—just not clickable ones.

Allowing easy navigation

AN EFFECTIVE STRUCTURE CAN BE NAVIGATED effortlessly if made visible. To this end, give the audience a map, tell them at all times where they are on the map, and tell them (when appropriate) where they can go with respect to the map.

Effective maps provide an immediate overview of the territory they chart. They usually include a strong visual component. In written documents, readers should see the tree structure at a glance in a table of contents before reading the first word. In Web sites, this table of contents, often called a site map, can be a two-dimensional diagram instead of a vertical list. In oral presentations, the preview can be shown on a slide, besides being spoken and perhaps underlined with gestures.

To provide an immediate overview, a map should be visible as a whole. As a counterexample, a table of contents running on several (double) pages offers partial views but no overview. Maps, however, need not display the complete depth: they can be limited to the top two levels, such as chapters and sections; each chapter can then include a local map, listing its sections and its subsections—not unlike road maps at different scales.

No matter how many pages it appears on in the end, too detailed a table of contents is hard for readers to process globally and, especially, to remember in a form that helps them navigate the document. Two levels is probably all they can absorb at first, even though a document can have up to three levels. For an oral presentation, subtract one everywhere: up to two levels in the tree, and one in the preview.

Audience members need to be reassured about where they are. Because they may wonder about it at any time, let them know at all times, for example in a running footline in a document. When it is impractical to do so at all times, as in oral discourse, let them know often, so they never have to wait long for help, should they feel lost at any time. To tell them where they are, use the same wording (or identifying picture) as on the map.

... protected by copyright.

... protected by copyright (see Terms of use for information on authorized reproduction).

A cryptic hyperlink: where does it lead?

A better hyperlink: it refers to the map and allows a better informed decision.

In written documents, audience members must also be told where they can go, as in a cross-reference in a paper document or a hyperlink on a Web site. So they can orient themselves and visualize their itinerary, indicate possible destinations like locations, with the same wording or picture as on the map. Provide whatever information will allow informed decisions.

Is it not better to have the message as a climax, so as to maintain the interest of the audience?

Professional audiences listen to presentations or read documents chiefly because they hope to find in this way the information they need. They easily lose patience when what they read or listen to does not seem relevant to them, all the more so when they are pressed by time. Hence, they have little tolerance for suspense, at least whenever it lasts longer than an instant. Presenting last what an audience wants to know first or most of all is more likely to make them *lose* interest. Details acquire their full relevance and significance in the light of the conclusion.

Keeping the audience interested is not a purpose in itself, really; getting the message across is, and this does not require forcing the audience to read or listen to everything. If they "buy it" early, they need not go on reading or listening to the supporting details for us to be successful.

A message placed early has a practical benefit, too: if audience members must stop reading or listening at any time, they will more likely have read or have heard our message already.

Must I not detail everything I have carried out if only so others can reproduce my experiment?

In scientific publications, whatever experiments help support the conclusions must indeed be described in enough detail to allow replication. Still, *enough detail* does not mean every detail: it means every *relevant* detail. These details need moreover not stand in the way. Because they seldom, in themselves, convey messages, they can often be relegated to an appendix or, for a presentation, to a companion document.

Building from the top down

As a rule, identify your message(s) early, not only for your audience within a given written document or oral presentation but also, first of all, for yourself when designing this document or this presentation. If you do not quite know what you are heading for, you have no relevant way to select what to include and what to leave out: you will likely include more than what is necessary to get your message across. Identifying the message at the end of the process and relocating it upfront is better than leaving it at the end (or, worse, including no message at all), but it does not promote careful content selection.

Top-down approach applied to an oral presentation

1 **Main message**   What you want your audience to remember

2 **Main points** What supports this message

3 **Subpoints**

Ask yourself first, *If my audience is to remember only one sentence from my entire oral presentation, what must it be?* The answer is your main message. Repeat the question at each level, broadening out as you go down (a few sentences, instead of one).

The top-down strategy works for entire documents or presentations and also for individual paragraphs or slides. Identify the message that the paragraph or the slide must convey; then—and only then—select the information and format that will convey this message optimally (instead of first developing the exact contents of the paragraph or slide, then searching for a suitable message to tack on to it).

Stating messages first

A N EFFECTIVE STRUCTURE PRESENTS MATERIAL in the order in which the audience is most likely to want to learn it, thus minimizing the navigation required—or the impatience of an audience who cannot navigate, as in oral presentations. It presents first what the audience is primarily interested in and afterwards what is less important or less urgent to them. It presents separately what fewer of them will want to know (perhaps in a companion document for an oral presentation).

Motivation	Make the audience receptive to the topic of the document
Message	Once you have their attention, tell them your main message
Details	Next, support this message: tell them how you got there
Appendix	Last of all, present separately what fewer will want to know

Professional audiences want to be told the message (that is, the *so what*) early, though not without proper motivation first, for messages make little sense out of context. They usually have little patience for "detective stories" that do not reveal the bottom line until the end. The details of an investigation are indeed largely irrelevant until we know the outcome of it. In other words, a chronological structure reporting work done in the order in which it was done, with conclusions at the end, works poorly: it focuses on the authors, not on the audience. An effective sequence presents first the motivation (the *why*), then the main message(s), and finally the details of the work.

A useful model, one that breaks the chronological paradigm, is that of mathematicians. When reporting their work, these normally present their conclusion first, calling it a theorem, then detail their hard work for those interested. In doing so, they strive to limit the details to whatever is strictly needed to prove the theorem, giving preference to the most elegant (that is, the simplest) proof of all. Thus a report is not a story of the work: it needs neither narrate every detail of the work nor report events in the sequence in which these took place.

The theorem–proof sequence is a useful model at all levels, not only for entire written documents or oral presentations, but also for single paragraphs or slides: these can usefully state a message upfront, then develop it verbally or visually, respectively—a prototypical way of getting messages across.

Prose is architecture,
not interior decoration,
and the Baroque is over.

— Ernest Hemingway

Effectiveness of assertion
is the alpha and omega of style.

— G. Bernard Shaw

Effective written documents

WRITTEN DOCUMENTS are valuable references. Although documents may well remain unread, they can also be reread many times or be read at the most convenient moment for each reader. In a context where many media compete for the attention of the readers, documents must allow each reader to assimilate effortlessly just what he or she needs to know. Their essential quality is therefore to be readable, that is, clear, accurate, and concise.

An effective way to go from scratch to a complete document proceeds iteratively in five steps. First, plan your document: gather your thoughts about the writing task. Second, design it: organize your material into a clear, well-structured hierarchy. Third, draft it: turn your ideas into paragraphs and sentences. Fourth, format it: take care of the visual component. Finally, revise it: test it and improve it iteratively until it is optimal, that is, the most effective it can be, given certain constraints.

Fundamentals

The name of the game
The three laws of communication
A thousand words, a thousand pictures
Chains and magical numbers
Trees, maps, and theorems

Effective written documents

Planning the document —————————————— Defining your purpose
Designing the document   Identifying your audience(s)
Drafting the document   Selecting your content
Formatting the document
Revising the document

Effective oral presentations

Planning the presentation
Designing the presentation
Creating slides
Delivering the presentation
Answering questions

Effective graphical displays

Understanding pictures
Planning the graph
Designing the graph
Constructing the graph
Drafting the caption

Applications

Effective instructions
Effective electronic mail
Effective Web sites
Effective meeting reports
Effective scientific posters

Planning the document

PLANNING IS THINKING about what we are to create. It thus means distancing ourselves from the situation and making sure we know everything we need to know in order to write an effective document. It is best carried out looking out our window, not staring at a text-processor one.

One systematic way to think about the document is to answer a set of questions about it. An effective and mnemonic set, unsurprisingly, consists of the five basic interrogative words starting with the letter *w*: *why*, *who*, *what*, *when*, and *where*. (The sixth interrogative *how*, conveniently not starting with *w*, is not an initial question: it points to the strategy, determined later on the basis of the answers to the other five questions.)

The five planning questions are not equally hard to answer. The constraints of time and space (*when* and *where*), critical as they are, are often easy to identify. Harder to determine are the purpose (*why*), the audience (*who*), and the content needed to reach this purpose with this audience (*what*). These three are tightly linked: the purpose expresses what the audience should (be able to) do after reading the document's content.

Planning need not take long but should be done with care, because it has a far-reaching impact. Poor planning results in unnecessary iterations before the writing process converges on the optimal document—when it has time to converge at all before the resources are up—and may result in writer's block (the inability to proceed with writing). The less time we have in total, the fewer iterations we can afford, and consequently the more time we should devote, proportionally, to planning.

When unclear initial ideas about the document to be created make planning hard, a possible strategy is to start drafting at once, in order to clarify our ideas. Sooner or later, though, we will need to go through the planning and designing steps, and to adapt our draft accordingly—an unavoidable iteration.

The five planning questions

Why	Purpose
Who	Audience
What	Content
When	Time constraints
Where	Space constraints

Should the purpose always be identified first?

Because it plays a deciding role, the purpose is often best identified first. Still, sometimes you know you need to react toward someone before deciding exactly what you want to reach, in which case you have identified your audience before determining your document's purpose.

I often have difficulties identifying my purpose. Any suggestions to make this process easier?

If you are writing a document at the request of someone (client, boss, etc.), ask this person what he or she identifies as the purpose for it. Placing the document in a broader framework helps, too. Is it, for example, part of a project? If yes, how is the document contributing to it?

When the purpose seems difficult to identify, an effective approach is simply to talk about it with someone else, such as a direct colleague. Talking out loud obliges one to turn thoughts into words, making them easier to work with. Your colleague will probably ask you questions, too, which will catalyze your thought process, and he or she might actually suggest a purpose.

What if I am convinced that the document I have been asked to write serves no purpose?

If you are deeply convinced that the document will make no difference, today or in the future, take up the issue with whoever has requested it, explaining that you can hardly write effectively without a clear idea of the document's purpose. (If the document is a contractual requirement, but you suspect that no one will ever read it, do write it, but do not spend much time on it.)

Common shortcomings

A communication purpose is more than a reason for writing: it gives a direction, suggests a strategy, provides a metric for success by enabling authors to visualize the outcome of the communication act.

A first typical shortcoming, then, is simply writing a document without having a clear purpose in mind. Indeed, many authors do have a reason for writing (*because my boss told me to report my research*) but do not visualize any potential or desired action on the part of the audience. The reason for writing can be confused with personal motivation, such as *I want to make an original contribution to science*, which can of course be a worthwhile pursuit in itself but does not constitute a communication purpose, because it does not involve the audience in any way. It is perhaps a motivation for carrying out the work but not for reporting on the work thus carried out.

Rational minds who do understand that a purpose for writing involves the audience may still fall short of identifying an observable outcome as part of it. They seem content with reaching the second step (*I want my audience to understand how it works*) and do not anticipate any action for the audience. The question these people might ask themselves is, *why do I want them to understand how it works?* Or perhaps, *how will I see that they understood?* That is, *what will this understanding in fact achieve?*

Finally, some otherwise clearly identified purposes may lead to ineffective communication strategies. Such is the case of purposes focusing on what are symptoms of excellence rather than sources of it (*I want my audience to be entertained by my text*) or expressing personal and often hidden agendas (*I want my boss to be impressed with my writing*). While these may well reflect legitimate aspirations, they offer no guarantee of helping authors reach a more fundamental professional purpose, namely get the audience to (be able to) act upon messages.

Defining your purpose

PURPOSES ARE THE ONLY METRIC against which to gauge the effectiveness of documents. A document is effective to the extent that it reaches its purpose—period. Accordingly, we can hardly determine the most suitable writing strategy without first having identified a purpose for our document. This purpose simply captures the change that the document is to produce: what must be different after it has been read? All communication is purpose-driven and, unsurprisingly, this purpose is defined in relation to both audience and author.

Effective purposes focus on the audience. They identify, not what the author should achieve, but rather what the readers should (be able to) do as a result of reading the document. This potential action may be understood broadly as anything involving the audience actively, even if only intellectually. Still, expressing it in observable terms helps envision a strategy: it is thus more useful to say we want the audience to *be able to disassemble the device* or to *sign the contract* rather than to *understand* or to *agree*, which cannot be observed as such. Audience-centered purposes moreover anticipate the purpose that readers bring to the communication: why will they read?

Although audience-centered, purposes acquire full meaning only in relation to an author. When identifying your purpose, identify your role in the communication: answer the question *who am I in relation to both my purpose and my audience?* or *why am I the person writing this document?* The audience will likely want to know, so be prepared to clarify it for them.

The purpose is implicit in the idea of getting messages across, defined as getting our audience to pay attention, understand, and (be able to) act upon our messages: it is the ultimate step. The first two steps, by contrast, are mere means to this end. For example, getting our audience to read a whole document is not a purpose in itself: if they (are able to) do what we want them to do without reading every word, so much the better.

Technical terms are not jargon

Since technical terms are so useful, how about using them for nonspecialists, too, but adding a glossary as an appendix to the document?

Readers can assimilate only so many new terms at a time, so beware of introducing too many. A glossary can certainly help, but it is best used redundantly: the (few) new terms must still be introduced in the text. If you include a glossary, let readers know about it, lest they never see it.

Is every reader really either a specialist or a nonspecialist?

As with all dichotomies, dividing the readers in just two groups is simplistic, and specialism is obviously a continuum that can be divided into as many groups as called for. For example, you might want to place your direct supervisor midway between specialists and nonspecialists: probably not quite as specialized as you are while still more specialized than most readers. Thinking in terms of just two groups, however, is a useful basis for reasoning about audiences.

For specialists, must I include conclusions? They can draw these themselves, right?

Readers as specialized as you are should be able to draw conclusions as well as you do, indeed. Of course, just because they can does not mean they will: interpretation is seldom trivial. Also, few readers are in as good a position as you are to interpret your own findings. It is therefore more constructive to include your conclusion and let the readers specialized enough to have an opinion on this conclusion disagree with it if they choose to. At least, you provided a basis for their thinking—and perhaps for a dialogue.

Technical terms are not the same thing as jargon. Defined in technical dictionaries, they are meant to make the document clear, accurate, and concise for as many readers as possible (within specialists). Jargon, by contrast, always reduces the readership to a "chosen few." It can happen purely by accident, such as when new employees unknowingly pick up company-specific terms and use these elsewhere. More often, though, it is caused by careless writing or, worse, by a desire to impress rather than help.

The 040 has a built-in 882.

The Motorola processor 68 040 has a built-in floating-point unit 68 882.

Technical terms are explicit, while jargon is cryptic. In the sentence *The 040 has a built-in 882*, readers who do not know what an 040 is would probably not know where to look for an explanation either. In the revised sentence, less specialized readers might of course not understand *floating-point unit*, but at least they have an idea of what the author is talking about (part of a processor) and they can also look for a definition in a technical dictionary.

Unexplained abbreviations easily become jargon: they needlessly exclude those readers who would understand the spelled-out form (including those who used to know this form and can use a reminder). Moreover, even a well-known acronym may expand to distinct meanings. Does *IP* stand for *intellectual property* or *Internet protocol*? Or *intraperitoneal*? Despite the presence of contextual clues, readers who readily recognize one meaningful expansion may not immediately think of the alternative ones (assuming that they are even aware of alternatives) and may therefore be misled, even if temporarily.

Identifying your audience(s)

Content

Specialists

Want more detail
Master technical terms

Nonspecialists

Need more background
and more interpretation

Need nontechnical terms
or defined technical ones

AUDIENCES ARE MULTIPLE, for each reader is unique. Still, readers can usefully be classified in broad categories on the basis of their proximity both to the subject matter (the *content*) and to the overall writing situation (the *context*). The challenge lies not so much in addressing a given category as in dealing with a mixed audience. The strategy is twofold: identify which part of the audience matters for your purpose and, for written documents, layer the information presented, so each reader can access only what is relevant to him or her.

Although knowledge forms a continuum, readers can usually be placed in one of two groups: those who already know much about the subject matter (*specialists*) and those who know little about it (*nonspecialists*). Clearly, specialism is relative: everyone is a specialist on some subjects and a nonspecialist on others. Moreover, even a group of all specialists could be subdivided into more specialized and less specialized readers. As with any structure, the two groups are a view of the mind.

Specialists and nonspecialists differ in the type of information they are primarily interested in. Specialists want more detail: they can understand the technical aspects, can often use these in their own work, and require them anyway to be convinced. Nonspecialists need more basic information to bridge the gap between what they know and what the document discusses: more background at the beginning, to understand the need for and importance of the work; more interpretation at the end, to understand the relevance and implications of the findings.

Specialists and nonspecialists differ as well in the vocabulary they master: specialists readily understand technical terms; nonspecialists do not. Technical terms, whenever appropriate, are effective: they are both precise and concise, and they help present the author as a specialist, thus enhancing credibility. For nonspecialists, they should be replaced by paraphrases or, if they are particularly desirable, be carefully introduced.

Are primary readers specialists and secondary readers nonspecialists?

The two audience typologies are independent; that is, primary readers can be nonspecialists and secondary ones specialists. For example, most executives are not (or no longer) specialists of all that they read about as primary readers. Conversely, specialists (re)reading a document in the future are definitely secondary readers.

By definition, I am writing for primary readers, so why should I worry about secondary ones?

Above all, worry about the readers who matter for you to reach your purpose. A quick reply sent by electronic mail may acceptably include little or no context, because secondary readers are generally few and probably unimportant. In contrast, a document that is worth archiving is one for which secondary readers do matter. Contextual information for secondary readers is usually a useful reminder for primary ones, too. In general, then, documents can usefully address both primary and secondary readers.

To address secondary readers, how about simply referring to a previous document?

Referring to a previous document as a sole way of providing context is hardly reader-friendly: it obliges readers to find this document first and to search through it for whatever context they might need to understand the document they actually want to read—an ill-defined task. Most readers will therefore not bother to do so, hence their understanding will be suboptimal. Such a reference is best provided redundantly, for those interested in more context or history.

Writing for a mixed audience is always a challenge: we must give to the secondary readers information that we assume the primary readers know already. How to do so, yet keep these readers interested? The solution, conceptually, is simple: just ensure that each sentence makes an interesting statement, one that is new to all readers—even if it includes information that is new to secondary readers only. This approach is illustrated in the example below, in which a few words of clarification go a long way.

We worked with IR.

A statement involving an unexplained abbreviation is cryptic for secondary readers who do not know what *IR* is and are left to wonder about its nature: is it a chemical, a computer code, "infrared", etc.?

We worked with IR. IR stands for Information Resources and is a new department.

Clarifying IR in an independent sentence, however, may be regarded as patronizing by primary readers. These then exclaim, *Hey, I know that!* when reading the second sentence, which tells them nothing new.

We worked with the recently launched Information Resources (IR) department.

A sentence that is appropriate for all readers states something new to all, while including information that is new to some and a useful reminder to others. Secondary readers thus learn about IR. Presumably, primary readers know what IR is but may not have in the front of their mind that this department was "recently launched". While not telling them anything they do not know, these two words will put them in a certain frame of mind for their further reading.

Context

Primary readers

Are close to the situation
both in space and in time

Secondary readers

Are reading far from here
or in the future from now

Require context to be able
to comprehend the issue

Quoting the original information
when replying to electronic mail
is one example of context used
as reminder for primary readers
while informing secondary ones.
Such quotes are best kept short
(the minimum needed to remind
readers of the point addressed).

Besides proximity to the subject matter, readers can be sorted on the basis of their proximity to the situation (the context), both in space and in time. Those close to the *here and now* are *primary readers*; any other ones are *secondary readers*. Clearly again, everyone is a primary reader on some matters and a secondary one on others, depending on their situation.

Primary readers are usually well-defined: they are the people we have in mind when we are writing the document. They are the ones expected to (be able to) act about the content of it and are thus listed under *to* in the header of short documents or electronic mail. Typical primary readers are our direct boss or colleagues, or our contact person at a client organization.

Secondary readers, on the other hand, are often ill-defined: they are the people who are sent a document for information (as listed under *copy to* or *cc*), but also those who obtain it via unpredictable routes, for example from a primary reader or from a library or archive. Typical secondary readers are distant colleagues, higher hierarchy, other people at a client's, or simply whoever will read the document in a few months or a few years (including, very often, the authors themselves).

To be understandable to both primary and secondary readers, documents must include context. Primary readers, who are close to the *here and now*, normally know the context but may not be thinking of it when starting to read; they benefit from a reminder, bringing it back to the front of their mind. Secondary readers, by contrast, are not (or no longer) aware of the context, so they need to find it in the document itself.

Context upfront not only broadens a document's readership, it is also essential for "getting our audience to pay attention": well phrased, it (re)establishes the importance of the subject and usefully prepares primary and secondary readers alike for the story told by putting them in a desired frame of mind.

Turning the story around

Why must I be selective in a written document? Readers can select what they want to read.

You should admittedly be even more selective for an oral presentation than for a document. Still, unnecessary material dilutes the message. Moreover, lengthy documents are intimidating enough that their reading may be postponed (*I will read this big report... when I have time*), even when only small part of them, such as the executive summary, must in fact be read. Should you nonetheless include much material, do give your readers the means to be selective by providing adequate navigational features. Just because readers need not read everything does not mean they know what they must read.

I am writing an article for a scientific journal: is my audience not made of specialists only?

Readers of scientific literature can be regarded as specialists indeed. Specialization, however, is relative, and few readers are as specialized as the authors, who usually studied the topic in great depth. Beware, therefore, of thinking that all readers already know what you know. Among less specialized readers are newcomers to the field, notably young doctoral students; people involved in multidisciplinary research, who are for example specialists of a technique but not of all the fields in which it is applied; and people having to review numerous papers or abstracts across a given field, as when serving on the program committee of a large conference.

Underestimating one's audience is not better than overestimating it, but it is less frequent. Broadening a document's readership without sacrificing accuracy is a worthwhile endeavor for scientific papers as for other documents.

Deciding what to include in a document and what to leave out is difficult, especially when reporting on a large body of work. To select content effectively, we must first identify our main messages, that is, the conclusions of our work. Most people, however, draw conclusions as they are writing: expressing their thoughts into words catalyzes their thinking. Alas, this approach is all but selective: the authors are writing for themselves, not for their audience.

Typically, authors proceed in chronological fashion.

First of all, they describe almost everything they have carried out as part of the work they report on.

Next, they write down everything they have obtained as a result of carrying out the work described.

As a final step, they think about what they can conclude from it all (what readers want to know most).

A more selective approach to deciding what content to include in a report turns the chronology around.

First, figure out your conclusions, that is, select the main messages to be conveyed to your audience.

Then, determine which findings are both necessary and sufficient to support your main messages.

Finally, decide in how much detail to describe the part of your work that led to the findings reported.

Selecting your content

CONTENT SHOULD BE LIMITED to whatever material serves the purpose and should be organized in a way that suits the audience. In other words, we should be highly selective, including only the material needed, not all material available. Being selective requires having a clear vision before writing. If we do not, we may well have to write the document twice: once for ourselves, to figure out our main messages, and once for our audience, to get these messages across effectively.

Audiences are seldom, if ever, homogeneous: they combine specialists and nonspecialists, primary and secondary readers. Effective documents, therefore, elegantly address all of these: they provide enough detail for the specialists while enabling any nonspecialist to understand the motivation for the work and the outcome of it; they satisfy the needs of the readers *here and now* and of those far from *here* or years from *now*.

The key to addressing mixed audiences in a written document is structure. At their most global level (their *macrostructure*), effective documents place first the parts that most readers are interested in, then those parts that only knowledgeable and interested readers will read. At the most detailed level (the *microstructure*), effective sentences carefully interlace new material with known material, to offer enough to readers who know less without appearing patronizing to the others.

Effective documents for any audience also take into account the purpose that readers bring to the communication. Thus they anticipate and answer the questions that these readers are likely to have, not only by including the right information but also by presenting this information in the right sequence. These questions may not match the ones we have as authors. In describing work we did, for example, we may be interested in the *how* when readers want to know the *why*, *who*, and *what*. We may thus want to clarify why we did the work, including perhaps who asked us or in what capacity we decided to do it.

Fundamentals

> The name of the game
> The three laws of communication
> A thousand words, a thousand pictures
> Chains and magical numbers
> Trees, maps, and theorems

Effective written documents

> Planning the document
> **Designing the document** ──────────────┐ Breaking the chronological model
> Drafting the document   │ Including a global component
> Formatting the document   │ Designing fractal documents
> Revising the document

Effective oral presentations

> Planning the presentation
> Designing the presentation
> Creating slides
> Delivering the presentation
> Answering questions

Effective graphical displays

> Understanding pictures
> Planning the graph
> Designing the graph
> Constructing the graph
> Drafting the caption

Applications

> Effective instructions
> Effective electronic mail
> Effective Web sites
> Effective meeting reports
> Effective scientific posters

Designing the document

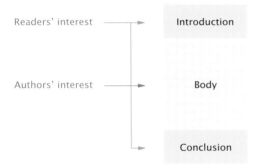

Readers' interest ——→ Introduction

Authors' interest ——→ Body

Conclusion

P LACING FIRST what readers are primarily interested in: there lies the foundation of effective document design. Readers, however, have other interests than authors: there lies the explanation for so many ineffective documents. Effective documents are audience-oriented, not self-centered.

Authors all too often report their work in a chronological way. They present the motivation for the work in an introduction (the *before*), detail this work in a body (the *during*), and report its outcome in a conclusion (the *after*). In this way, they match the work process closely, often all the way to the relative time spent on each part: many authors spend much time writing the body of their reports or articles, exactly like they spent much time carrying out the work, but devote comparatively little time to writing both the introduction and the conclusion.

Readers, in contrast, are primarily interested in the motivation for the work and in the outcome of it, not in the work itself. First of all, they need to relate the work to a broader context much more than they need to understand how it was done, all the more so if they are nonspecialists or secondary readers. Next, they want to know how they are affected by this work, that is, what the findings of the work mean in their own case. In a chronological document, they thus read the introduction, then often go straight to the conclusion, skipping the body. Specialists might later read (parts of) the details in this body, if only to convince themselves of the validity of the conclusion.

A chronological structure, in other words, is straightforward for authors but suboptimal for readers: it requires navigation. Effective document designs, therefore, break the chronology: they place first what the readers are primarily interested in. This first component also provides readers with a global view that helps them assimilate details, should they read (parts of) the body. Such a global component can usefully be included in front of more detailed material at any level in the document.

Designing short and long documents

Short and long documents alike usefully include a global component that makes sense on its own, whether or not it is redundant with any other part.

Body

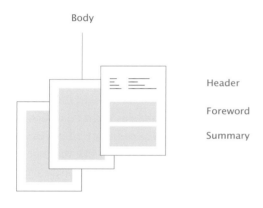

Header

Foreword

Summary

Introduction   Appendices

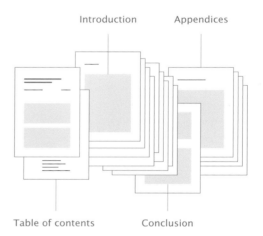

Table of contents   Conclusion

When the document is short (a few pages, perhaps) and addresses a homogeneous audience, it need not be abstracted: the foreword would not differ sufficiently from the introduction, whether in extent or in technicality, and neither would the summary from the conclusion; in each case, one of the two is enough. Still, the document can usefully present the material in the order in which readers want it, with the motivation for and outcome of the work upfront—together with the header on the first page. You can think of the resulting structure equivalently as having an abstract but neither an introduction nor a conclusion or as having, in fact, no abstract but a conclusion placed right after the introduction. Either way, what follows the first page is the body.

A multipage letter can include a global component, too, and be signed at the bottom of the first page, with more detailed material on subsequent pages, perhaps each with its own heading. You can choose to think of it as a one-page letter with attachments instead of a multipage letter, but the idea remains.

When the document is longer than just a few pages and all the more so when it is supposed to address a mixed audience of specialists and nonspecialists (two conditions that are frequently met in practice), it does benefit from including a redundant abstract. Indeed, the introduction and conclusion are likely too long to constitute a useful global component and too technical for the less specialized readers. A distinct global component, made of a foreword and a summary inspired by (but not copied from) the introduction and conclusion, will tell all readers what they want to know first of all and most of all. Ideally, it fits on the very first page, with the header.

Although documents may display the abstract as one block of text so as to be economical with paper, they should nonetheless include both motivation and outcome in it, that is, the *before* and the *after*.

Breaking the chronological model

THE READERS' PRIMARY INTEREST in the *before* and *after* suggests two strategies for effective design. First, devote sufficient time to drafting the introduction and conclusion, for these parts are typically read first of all and most of all. Second, order the material, not *chrono*logically, but logically, that is, in the order in which readers are most likely to read it.

A chronological story can be made reader-friendly in two ways. One way is to relocate the conclusion after the introduction, before the body; this solution works best for short documents and for homogeneous audiences, such as nonspecialists only. Another way is to maintain the chronological structure as is but to precede it with a component that restates, in a concise and somewhat different way, what readers want to know first, as a form of effective redundancy most appropriate for longer or more complex documents, addressing mixed audiences.

Short or long, documents can thus usefully include a global, stand-alone component, stating upfront the motivation for and outcome of the work. Accordingly, this global component, known under such names as *abstract* or *executive summary*, comprises two parts: the *before*, usually known as *foreword*, and the *after*, usefully named *summary* in a restricted sense. These two parts vary widely in absolute and relative lengths from document to document, even if they are best kept short. An abstract, in other words, is all but a condensed full story: in a sense, it reports the starting point and the end point only.

Global components serve many purposes. By telling the story in a compact, audience-oriented way, they are the only parts that most readers need to read: they thus save these readers much time and effort. For those readers who end up reading the whole document, they provide the necessary framework to understand and mentally structure the subsequent details. For all potential readers, they are a powerful selection tool: they help them decide whether to read (parts of) the document.

Short document
Relocate material

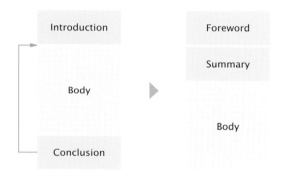

Longer document
Restate material

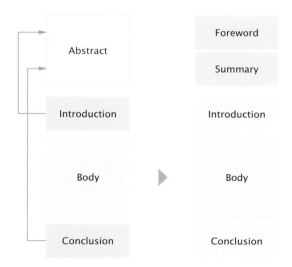

Is the foreword identical to the introduction?

The foreword has exactly the same structure as the introduction, but it is normally shorter and also less specialized than the introduction. It must indeed be understandable to all readers, including less specialized ones. These readers, typically executives, may have different stakes in the need than the specialists. This difference is reflected in the foreword and introduction.

If it seems hard to write a foreword that differs from the introduction by being either shorter or less technical, you might apply the strategy for short documents: in place of an abstract, relocate the conclusion after the introduction.

How can I write an abstract for documents that are in essence detailed, such as minutes of a meeting, specifications, or procedures?

The foreword should pose no specific problem: it accounts for both the document and the work that led to it, as usual. For example, it explains why a meeting was needed, who called it, etc.

The summary can in this case best be regarded as what the audience needs to know most of all or what will help them understand the details. For a meeting, it includes decisions and actions. For specifications (and for similar documents), it might be what is new or special about them, or simply an overview of the device specified.

Is an objective the same as a need?

An objective is half a need only: it corresponds to the desired situation but does not capture the actual one. As such, it fails to justify a task.

Equivalent terms

The proposed model of global component (abstract) is applicable to almost any professional document reporting some "work done" in the broadest sense. Because it builds on the universal interest shown by professionals in the motivation for and outcome of the piece of work reported, it is just as effective for a business report as for a scientific publication. Still, it is traditionally called or described differently by different professional or even corporate cultures. Below are equivalent terms frequently encountered.

Abstract (the generic term used here) is often used in academic writing but less so in the business world, where a report's global component is usually called *executive summary*, because it enables executives (who are often less specialized) to make decisions. Scientists, engineers, and managers alike may also speak of an *extended summary*, usually to suggest that it encompasses both the motivation (foreword) and the outcome (summary in a restricted sense). A foreword is sometimes called *purpose statement*, because it justifies both the work and the document.

The items in the abstract have several names, too. You may prefer to think of the *need* as a *problem* or an *issue*, but these may be needlessly restrictive: the need may be an *opportunity*, too; furthermore, an intellectual need may be thought of as a *question*. A *task* requested by others can be called a *mission*; one focusing on the means more than on the people can be regarded as the *approach* or *method* used. The *object of the document* is sometimes labeled *rhetorical purpose* (although this term is also used for the foreword as a whole, resulting in confusion); when it announces the structure of the document, it can be regarded as an *overview* or as a *preview*. The *findings*, when numerical, are the *main results*. The *conclusion* is the *main message*, also known as *take-home message*, a term perhaps more used for oral presentations. Finally, the *perspectives* are also known as *future work* or perhaps *next steps*.

Including a global component

To TELL READERS what readers primarily want to know, abstracts include two parts: a foreword and a summary. The foreword, which is similar in nature to the introduction, focuses on the situation *before* the work was done. In contrast, the summary, which is similar in nature to the conclusion, focuses on the situation *after* the work. Effective abstracts include little or no information from the document's body.

The foreword accounts for both the work and the document. First, it states the need for the work reported, as a difference between the actual and desired situations, possibly preceded by whatever context helps understand this need better. Next, it states the task carried out, without detailing what was done. (Strictly speaking, because it corresponds to the *before* part, it states what the authors had decided or been asked to do; usually, this is what they actually did, too.) Finally, switching from a content point of view to a rhetorical one, it establishes the object of the document, that is, what the document does or covers, and possibly what the readers should do with it.

Foreword	Context	Why the need is so pressing or important
The *before*	**Need**	Why something needed to be done at all
	Task	What was undertaken to address the need
	Object	What the present document does or covers
Summary	**Findings**	What the work done yielded or revealed
The *after*	**Conclusion**	What the findings mean for the audience
	Perspectives	What the future holds, beyond this work

The summary states and, especially, interprets the outcome of the work. First, it mentions the findings or main results. Next, it clarifies what these findings mean, given the audience and the need. So doing, it may recommend a course of action for the audience to address the need. Beyond looking back at the need, it might look ahead and offer some perspectives.

What exactly is the difference between task and object? Can these not be combined?

Task and object differ in focus. Schematically, the task states what the authors did, whereas the object establishes what the document does. The first thus focuses on the work carried out; the second, on the communication of this work. Should you combine the two, focus on the task (*Therefore, we developed a new method to ...*), rather than on the object (*This paper presents a new method to ...*): the task follows the need more logically and clarifies who did the work. Also, beware of mixing up places and tenses, as in *In this report, we measure ...*, which makes no sense: you do not in fact measure anything in the report; you did so, presumably, in the lab.

What does the task become for a review paper?

As author of a review, you can regard your job as reporting the work of others, in which case you sum up this work, collectively, in the task (*Over the last twenty years, researchers have ...*), or as reporting your review work, in which case you state so in the task. The need, of course, must be adapted; in the second case, it must be the need for a review of research in the field.

Should a scientific abstract include an object?

The object of the document must orient readers as to the document's contents and structure, so they can decide whether (or what) to read. When it merely repeats what the need and task already state or clearly imply, it is best omitted. Such is often the case for experimental work, for which the body is predictably structured as *Materials and methods, Results, Discussion*.

Of the many ways to formulate tasks and objects, some are more logical or more readily recognized.

The task must clarify not only the work carried out but also the agents who carried it out. If these are the authors of the document (the most usual case), it is best phrased in the active voice and first person (*we measured, we developed, we implemented*, etc.). If not, as for a review paper, it is logically phrased in the third person, preferably in the active voice (*In recent years, researchers have investigated ...*), more informative and usually more readable than an impersonal construct (*... has been investigated*).

The task can be effectively connected to the need by a phrase before the subject. A simple *therefore* is usual enough, but the desired part of the need is often an elegant option (*To increase the speed, we redesigned ...*). This initial phrase can be used to clarify any requesting party, too (*At the request of the Senior Management Team, we redesigned ...*).

The object, in contrast, focuses not on the authors but on the document itself. Thus, it can best use the document as grammatical subject of the clause (*This report summarizes, This paper presents*, etc.). Such a phrasing is equally appropriate for objects of parts of the document (*Chapter 3 compares ...*).

Task and object differ also in the tenses they use. The task, like all references to the work carried out, is best set in the past (or the present perfect) tense. The object, like all references to actual documents, is atemporal and thus best set in the present tense.

Whereas choosing a grammatical subject for a task or an object is straightforward (*we, this report*, etc.), selecting a suitable verb for it is more challenging. Did we *examine, analyze*, or perhaps *investigate*? Does the document *present, explain*, or *report on*? The verb, not the subject, carries the strength here.

Thinking in concentric layers

Abstracts can be thought of as made of four concentric layers. At the center is "communication", a rhetorical layer focusing on the document. Around this rhetorical layer is a "work done" layer, consisting of the task (*before*) and the findings (*after*). It focuses on the authors, who usually have carried out the task and generated the findings. Around this "work done" layer is a "problem-solution" layer, comprising the need (*before*) and the conclusion (*after*). This one focuses on the readers, who, presumably, are concerned by the need and must have the findings interpreted, in view of this need. Finally, around this "problem-solution" layer is an optional "situation" layer, comprising the context (*before*) and the perspectives (*after*). It focuses neither exclusively on the readers nor exclusively on the authors (perspectives might involve either of them); in a sense, this is an "anyone" (or an "everything else") layer.

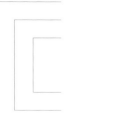

Context	Anyone	
Need	Readers	*What you want ≠ what you have*
Task	Author(s)	*What I/we did to address the need*
Object	Document	*What the document does/covers*
Findings	Author(s)	*What I/we found, doing the task*
Conclusion	Readers	*What these findings mean to you*
Perspectives	Anyone	

Established from a chronological point of view (*before/after*), the abstract in two distinct parts can easily be reinterpreted in terms of the motivation (the *why*) and outcome (the *what*). The first part (the *before*) might be known to some readers, for these might well have pointed out the need and ordered the task, so the news appears in the second part (the *after*). Still, the first part not only informs those who did not know, it also prepares those who did to assimilate the message(s) optimally, by reminding them of the context and of the need, thus placing both the task and the document in perspective.

The need is well known to my audience.
Should I still include it in the document?

A need is bound to a point in space and time. It might be known to primary readers, but not to secondary ones. Moreover, primary readers seldom have it in mind as they begin to read and might not see it the way the authors see it. A carefully stated need thus puts all readers in a favorable frame of mind for their reading.

The foreword part of the abstract establishes motivation and, to some extent, relationship. It always plays an important role. Of course, it can be brief or presented as already known, especially when the audience is clearly defined (it might start with *As you may remember, ...*).

Is having the motivation in the introduction
not enough? Why should it be in the abstract?

Whereas titles are the very first selection tool, abstracts are the main one. If an abstract fails to include motivation, readers are more likely to stop reading than to look for it elsewhere, such as in the introduction—all the more so when the abstracts are available free of charge, whereas the full documents must be purchased.

I must write an abstract limited to 100 words.
This is very short. Can I drop any item at all?

When the number of words is severely limited, condensing or combining items is preferable to suppressing any, for all of them play a role. When needed, context, need, and task can often be written as one sentence (*In the framework of ... and in an effort to ..., we investigated ...*). At times, the object can be expressed implicitly.

Common suboptimal abstracts

While any abstract missing one or more components is suboptimal, three types are particularly frequent: *promissory*, *out of the blue*, and *self-centered* ones.

Promissory	Out of the blue	Self-centered
Context		
Need		
Task		Task
Object		
	Findings	Findings
	Conclusion	
	Perspectives	

An abstract including the motivation (the *before*) but not the outcome (the *after*) is most frustrating: it promises but does not deliver, obliging readers who would have had enough with a good abstract to dig in the details in an effort to find the message. It is perhaps acceptable as a proposal submitted to a selection committee long before a conference but far less so as the abstract of a final document.

An abstract including the outcome (the *after*) but no motivation (the *before*) comes out of the blue. The findings, appearing first, are easily confused with context. Moreover, the conclusion is usually impossible to understand properly without a need. While it may seem acceptable to primary readers, well aware of the need and task, an out-of-the-blue abstract is cryptic for secondary ones, who are not.

An abstract that is limited to a task and findings, with no real motivation (need) and no real message (conclusion), is self-centered: it ignores that which the audience most wants to know. It makes them wonder what this document has to do with them, as well as what they are supposed to do about it.

Conveying the motivation and the outcome

The two key questions, *why* and *(so) what*, can be associated symbolically or mnemonically to the two parts of the abstract and, within these parts, to each item, with its respective slant.

The first part of the abstract implicitly answers the question *why* at every step. The context answers the question *why now*: it explains how the recent history and current situation led to the need. If reader-oriented, the need implicitly answers the question *why you*: by reading it, readers should perceive the document's relevance to them, that is, understand why it was sent to them or decide whether to select it for reading. In turn, the task implicitly answers the question *why me/us*, clarifying what the authors have to do with the stated need. Finally, the object answers the question *why this document*, that is, *given the need and the task, what are the document's purpose or contents? And what should we, readers, do with it?*

Why? Motivation	Context	Why now	My/our or your current situation
	Need	Why you	*Why this is in fact relevant to you*
	Task	Why me/us	*What I/we have got to do with it*
	Object	Why this document	
What? Outcome	**Findings**	What	*What resulted from the task done*
	Conclusion	So what	*What these findings mean to you*
	Perspectives	What now	*What I/we or you should do next*

The second part of the abstract similarly answers the question *what* at every step. Thus the findings merely state the *what*, that is, *what have I or we found by carrying out the task?* The conclusion (the message) answers the question *so what*, typical of readers who cannot guess whether some findings mean good news or bad news, or how good or how bad it is. Closing the outermost loop of the multiply nested structure, the perspectives, like the context, focus on temporal aspects and answer the question *what now* or, equivalently, *what next*.

What is wrong with a heavily technical abstract? If readers do not understand it, can they not see that they are not part of the intended audience?

Giving up on a document because one plainly does not understand is such a negative choice. Is it not infinitely more constructive to enable all potential readers to understand our abstract and, with this understanding, decide rationally whether they can benefit from the document?

Unlike the document, the abstract will be read by virtually all readers, be it as a selection tool. Consequently, a reader-friendly abstract is one that is understandable to the least specialized of our readers (while still useful to specialists).

Should I write the abstract first or last, that is, before or after writing the complete document?

Writing the abstract after the whole document usually makes for better abstracts. Writing it before the document, however, usually makes for better structured, more selective documents. Perhaps you can write abstracts first *and* last?

In a similar way, writing the introduction early typically makes, not for better introductions, but for better research, because it helps clarify, for the authors at this point, what they have, what they want, and how they hope to find it.

Must foreword and summary be labeled thus?

The foreword and the summary do not need to be labeled; neither, in fact, does the abstract. Global components, be they abstracts or other, are mainly identified as such by their location. Above all else, they must be in the right place.

Creating useful headers

Whatever the document is, the header must allow its correct routing, filing, and selection for reading or other processing, such as destruction. Readers mostly select on the basis of the title and author(s), so these should be prominent. Equally important yet too often absent in online documents is a date and, for unambiguous reference, a unique identifier, such as a reference number. This identifier should then appear on each page next to the page number, so the page can be traced even if it becomes loose.

The title of a report or of an article, or, equivalently, the *subject* of a memorandum or electronic mail, is a challenging element to write. To remain visual, it must be kept short—a question of visual length on paper or on the screen more than of word count. The question is, what do we tell in these few words?

Titles, like documents, can be structured effectively in two parts: a global one and a more specific one, perhaps separated by a dash or a colon, or written as a title and subtitle. The two parts work together like a funnel, gradually narrowing down the topic (*Project meeting on Fri 20 Apr: revised agenda*). Used in isolation, the first part would be too vague (what about the "project meeting on Fri 20 Apr"?) whereas the second one would lack its framework (the "revised agenda" for what meeting?). The titles of related documents can have the same first part and distinct second parts, making for easy sorting (*Project meeting on Fri 20 Apr: list of attendees*).

Whether the distribution list is part of the header is debatable. Clearly, it plays a role for selection, as when recipients want to know whether they are listed under *to* or under *cc*. In any case, it should not stand in the way of more important information. When it is long, it is best moved out of the header and onto a page of its own, inserted where it can easily be located without being overly prominent, such as after the first page—or after the last one.

Allowing informed decisions

The abstract, with its two parts, allows two decision moments. After reading the first part (the motivation), readers can gauge their interest for the topic and for the document. Only those who care enough about both will go on reading. After reading the second part (the message), they can normally take action about the need and, again, decide whether to quit or read on. This decision will be influenced by their confirmed interest but depends largely on their need for the details. Specialists typically want the details, either because they can use them in their own work or because they wish to assess the quality of the work done and, with it, the credibility of the message.

Header	Title		
Screening	Author(s)		
		Is this for me?	If *yes*, go on to the foreword
Foreword	Context		If *no*, then stop reading here
Motivation	**Need**		
	Task		
	Object		
		Do I care?	If *yes*, go on to the summary
Summary	**Findings**		If *no*, then stop reading here
Outcome	**Conclusion**		
	Perspectives		
		Do I need more?	If *yes*, go on to the document
			If *no*, then stop reading here

A very first selection tool, however, is the header preceding the abstract, specifically the document's title and author(s), and possibly the mention of the reader's name under *to* or *cc.* The global component of a document is thus best regarded as comprising three parts: header, foreword, and summary. For most documents, notably short to medium-length reports, the three parts together should ideally not exceed one page, as it increases the probability of their being read immediately. Having to turn a page seems to be quite a psychological barrier.

The context, limited in this case to a single sentence, is sufficient to situate the need in both time (April 2007) and space (Belgium). Next comes the need, presented as an opportunity, not a problem. All the same, it represents a gap between ABC's current situation and a more favorable alternative, which is desirable for the readers.

Given the audience of executives, the task is explicit on processes. The author's function (tax officer), normally indicated in the header, can justify that she went ahead and "prepared a rough estimate" but perhaps not that she engaged expenses for legal consultation, so the task clarifies that the CFO backed her. It also indicates who the consultant is, thus answering a possible question from the CEO.

The object of the document says not only what the report covers but also what the readers should do with it (prepare the meeting).

The summary in itself (findings, conclusion, perspectives) is set here as one solid paragraph, but, if longer, it could also be divided in two or three paragraphs, as is the case for the foreword above. Conversely, this foreword could be set as a single paragraph, too: at less than 200 words, it is still reasonably short. Which option is best (one paragraph or several) depends also on the page layout.

As of April 2007, the Belgian legislation authorizes VAT consolidation among the members of a group. Such a VAT group could be an opportunity for us at Amazing Belgian Chocolates and for our sister company Choc Export: our VAT payments could be used to offset their (notoriously slow) VAT refunds, positively affecting the cash flow of both companies. Filing a consolidated VAT return for the VAT group thus formed, however, would require that we adapt our accounting practices as well as our IT systems.

As a first step toward evaluating the benefit for us of forming a VAT group together with Choc Export, I prepared a rough estimate of the potential savings and, in agreement with our CFO, Linda Thielemans, I contacted a tax consultant at Van Belle & Partners to verify that ABC and Choc Export meet the criteria for constituting a VAT group under the new decree.

In preparation for our upcoming committee meeting on Wed 13 Jun, this note sums up my findings so far and maps out what I identify as the next three steps, to be discussed in committee and approved by you.

My rough estimate suggests consolidated savings in excess of 20 000 euros per year, and the reply from Van Belle & Partners is positive on all points. Accordingly, I recommend that we move forward with the project by carrying out these three tasks: (1) with the accounting teams of both companies, evaluate the required adjustments to the systems and the costs associated with implementing them; (2) if the anticipated savings exceed these costs, request authorization from the VAT administration; (3) once it is authorized, implement the VAT group.

Below is a possible abstract for a scientific article published in a journal (abstracts of research reports for internal use in an organization would be similar). Such an abstract addresses other researchers. Still, in an effort not to be needlessly technical, it limits acronyms to those strictly useful for conciseness: thus, it introduces *ILT* (which it uses three times), but it avoids *AAA* for *abdominal aortic aneurysm*, even though this acronym is used in the article itself.

Context—provides background for less specialized readers and, so doing, establishes or recalls the importance of the problem.

An aneurysm in the abdominal aorta will rupture as soon as the wall stress exceeds the wall strength at any location, thus threatening the patient's life. Elective surgical repair, however, is costly and risky. Evaluating wall stress to predict the risk of rupture is therefore essential toward patient management, yet current models suffer from several limitations. Among others, they do not consider the presence of an IntraLuminal Thrombus (ILT), a fibrin structure present in variable degrees in 75% of aneurysms. Using computed tomography and finite elements, we investigated whether the presence of ILT alters the distribution or the magnitude of the wall stress in aneurysms of the abdominal aorta. This paper reports the wall stress distribution in four patients and discusses the impact of the ILT configuration.

Need—motivates the audience by stating the difference between the desired and actual situations.

Task—states what the authors undertook to address the need, in the first person (*we*), past tense.

Object—clarifies what the paper covers without repeating the task, in the active voice, present tense.

In all four patients, the presence of an ILT altered the stress distribution and reduced the peak stress by 6 to 38% ($p = .067$), depending on the geometry. As a consequence, it should be taken into account in any patient-specific model of aortic aneurysms for evaluating the wall stress and the risk of rupture. Still, it may also adversely affect the wall strength and will therefore remain the focus of future work.

Findings—state the main results in a way that both less and more specialized readers find helpful.

Conclusion—interprets findings (states the *so what*)—in this case, all the way to a recommendation.

Perspectives—broaden the view with any further needs and tasks.

With just under 200 words, the above abstract can convey the motivation for and outcome of the work with some accuracy, without intimidating readers by its length. Still, and when allowed by the journal, it is best set in two paragraphs (foreword, summary). An abstract under 150 words is challenging to write; one over 250 words is seldom justified for an article.

Common shortcomings

Should every item at every level begin with a global component?

If an item constitutes a meaningful entity, surely there is something general to be said about it, before each of its constituent parts is detailed. At the very least, you can prepare the readers for the item's structure, even if this structure is already shown by a set of headings. Indeed, headings are often seen but not read. Moreover, they are not seen together when the item spans several pages, so they provide no global view.

Can the global component of a chapter or section be its first section or subsection?

The global component of a chapter or section is really a level above sections or subsections: it belongs to the chapter or section as a whole, so it is best placed directly under the heading of this chapter or section, before any heading of section or of subsection. (As a minor point, doing so results in a clearer page layout, too.)

Is an object still required when readers are used to a structure (for example, when it is identical to that of matching items in other documents)?

Primary readers might be used to a structure, but any secondary readers, almost by definition, cannot be: an object is thus a necessity for them and may be a useful reminder to other readers. However, avoid presenting as new something that is known to your readers, lest you appear patronizing. If the structure is usual, say so. For a section on *Results*, you might thus write *As usual, our results come from three areas: ....* You would list here the areas in question again, before discussing each of them in a subsection.

As a clear confirmation of the usefulness of telling the beginning of the story and the end of it together in one place, some scientific journals now require that authors announce their conclusion at the end of the introduction. Similarly, many authors start the conclusion section (at the end of the document) by restating the need, the task, or even the object of the document, which appear in the introduction. Introductions or conclusions structured in this way, while well-meant, needlessly duplicate the abstract. With a well-written abstract, readers are equipped for the complete article; the introduction should be limited to the *before*; the conclusion, to the *after*.

Even if deemed unnecessary as part of the abstract, the object of the document should certainly appear in the introduction, typically as a final paragraph starting with *This document is organized as follows* and then listing what each chapter or section covers, preferably in the active voice (*Chapter 2 reviews ...*). The chapters or sections, in turn, should include a global paragraph upfront, to orient the readers.

Two headings that follow each other immediately, such as those of Section 2.4 and Subsection 2.4.1, are usually an indication that a global paragraph is missing. At times, however, the first subsection is precisely what is needed for a global paragraph, so we can simply delete that subsection's heading (and, of course, renumber the subsequent headings). Usually, the heading thus deleted was of little use, as in *General description* or *Preliminary remarks*.

The presence of a paragraph between the heading of a section and that of its first subsection does not, in itself, guarantee an effective mental preparation of the readers for the structure ahead. In particular, such paragraphs often miss the *object of the section*, (the local equivalent of the object of the document), especially when they have been built by relocation of other items, rather than written for the purpose.

Designing fractal documents

E FFECTIVE DOCUMENT DESIGNS ARE FRACTAL. They exhibit an identical structure—global component, then details— for the whole document and for each of its constituent items at any level, such as the chapters, sections, and subsections, in fact all the way down to the level of individual paragraphs.

Like documents, chapters (or sections or subsections) should begin with a global component, perhaps just one paragraph, typically located before the heading of the first subbranch (for a chapter, before the first section). This global paragraph might contain any and all items of a foreword and summary. At the very least, it must include an object, preparing readers for the chapter's structure, but it can also usefully set forth a motivation for the chapter or the chapter's main messages.

Chronological chapters (or sections or ...) can often be turned into global–detailed ones in the same way that documents can. Any conclusion section, for example, can be moved upfront as part of the chapter's global component and be suppressed where it was—or for long chapters, be restated briefly upfront.

Drafting the document

CAREFULLY WRITTEN DOCUMENTS are reader-friendly, just like carefully designed software is user-friendly. They are simple and direct, trying to help the readers, not to impress or confuse them; in a word, they are readable. They not only contain the right information in the right place but also phrase this information in a way that is easy to read. Hence, they allow readers to spend as little time as possible on the text and as much of it as possible on the ideas expressed.

Readable written documents are clear, accurate, and concise. They carry a single, readily understandable meaning. They tell "the truth, the whole truth, and nothing but the truth." And they achieve clarity and accuracy in as few words as possible. Clarity, accuracy, conciseness (in that order) are the priorities at the level of the paragraphs, sentences, and individual words.

Text entities at different levels have different functions, hence they may require different approaches for optimal readability. Paragraphs convey messages, ideally in a stand-alone way: each paragraph thus states its message first, then develops it in theorem–proof fashion. Sentences state ideas, in one-to-one correspondence: short sentences can express simple ideas, while longer sentences are required for more complex ideas. Well-chosen words contribute to a clear, accurate, concise text.

Writing simply does not suggest simplifying the material but conveying the complexity of this material in the simplest way, something many of us have learned to do about mathematics. We thus have been taught to "simplify fractions", for example to replace $679/194$ by the more readable, yet equivalent $7/2$; we have seen the advantage of a change of coordinate system to describe an object or a phenomenon with simpler equations; we have been rewarded for deriving the "most elegant" proof of a theorem. Still, when useful, we know how to approximate, that is, to simplify the material to the desired level of accuracy, as when writing $\pi \approx 3.14$, which is in fact a correct statement.

Stating the message upfront

Must every paragraph convey a message?

Every paragraph must have a unifying theme (a reason for its sentences to be set together) and must serve the purpose of the document. Often, this theme is a message, but not always. An introductory paragraph, for example, may not hold a true message, expressing a *so what*. Conversely, a one-paragraph abstract typically comprises several messages, at various levels. Whether or not its theme can be considered a true message, each paragraph should orient the readers as to its content and its structure.

I find it difficult to ensure that each paragraph states a message upfront. Any suggestion?

As much as possible, determine what you want to say with each paragraph before you write it. You could even write all the first sentences first, that is, before writing the rest of any paragraph, as a way to envision the structure of a section. Together, these sentences answer the question, *what ideas must my audience remember here?*

After writing, you can inspect each paragraph. If the message is at the end, move it to the front, adjusting the paragraph as needed. If there is no message, question the paragraph's function.

Is there a maximum length for paragraphs?

Each paragraph should have whatever length it needs to develop its message appropriately. Some might be short—as short as one sentence, perhaps—while others are comparatively long. Long paragraphs can be visually intimidating, though; paragraphs that must get the attention of the audience are therefore best kept short.

Paragraphs that fail to clarify their topic upfront are frequently misleading. In the example below, the first two sentences suggest that the paragraph discusses "single-use, disposable medical devices," then the third sentence reveals that what it does, actually, is compare two types of medical devices.

> Single-use, disposable medical devices are packaged and sterilized by the manufacturer. Their packaging must provide protection, facilitate sterilization, maintain sterility, … Reusable devices, by contrast, must be …

> Medical devices may be broadly divided into two categories, disposable and reusable, having different sterilization requirements. Single-use, disposable devices are packaged and sterilized by the manufacturer. Their … Reusable devices, by contrast, must be …

More common than a missing topic is a message that appears too late and therefore lacks visibility. Such is typically the case in a paragraph structured chronologically with its conclusion at the very end, thus giving the proof before stating the theorem, or one postponing the *so what* until after the *what*, as when describing a figure before interpreting it.

> Figure 2 shows the evolution of the Ge content in the SiGe layer. Obviously there is a nearly linear decrease of the Ge content with increasing fluence. Knowing the …

> The germanium content decreases linearly with increasing fluence (Figure 2). Knowing …

Stating and developing messages

PARAGRAPHS ARE THE ESSENTIAL structuring components of the document: they appear even in short documents that are not otherwise divided into sections, such as letters. They retain document characteristics that sentences do not. First, paragraphs—like documents—tell a story of their own: effective paragraphs remain understandable even in isolation, whereas many otherwise effective sentences do not. Second, paragraphs convey messages: each states and develops one.

Paragraphs, like full documents, should remain meaningful (to a point, that is) even out of context. Each paragraph must have its reason for being, namely to convey a certain message. Conversely, each message usually deserves its own paragraph: one paragraph per message and one message per paragraph. Paragraph size then simply depends on message complexity: more complex messages typically require longer paragraphs. As with sections, the optimal granularity is also a question of balance between paragraph length and paragraph number: few long paragraphs are hard to read; so are many short ones. In most cases, a sequence of one-sentence paragraphs makes little structural sense: messages are stated but not developed.

Effective paragraphs, like effective documents (or chapters), state their message early, ideally as early as the first sentence. A well-written first sentence, not unlike a well-written abstract, enables the readers to decide whether to read the paragraph, by announcing its content and by suggesting its structure. With prominent key words, first sentences help the readers locate quickly the paragraphs that are most relevant to them or find again some information they remember having read. By reading the first sentence of every paragraph, the readers should be able to form a good idea of the document's content.

After stating its message, an effective paragraph develops it along an appropriate structure, typically revealed by the way in which the various sentences are connected to one another.

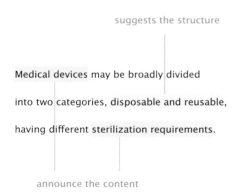

suggests the structure

Medical devices may be broadly divided
into two categories, disposable and reusable,
having different sterilization requirements.

announce the content

Need paragraphs always be parallel or serial?

Paragraphs need not always be entirely parallel or entirely serial. They may use a combination of the two structures, or be "pseudo-parallel," (lining up comparable yet not identical subjects). To be readable, however, they should not miss opportunities for a parallel or serial structure, such as introducing a switch in subject ($A \rightarrow C$) that does not reflect a switch in topic (yielding A–B C–A, instead of the parallel link A–B A–C) or positioning a new item (C) before an item (B) mentioned in the previous sentence (yielding A–B C–B, rather than the serial link A–B B–C).

Is the parallel structure not boring to read?

Parallelism may seem to encourage repetition. Not so, however: unpleasant repetitions must of course be removed lest they become noise, but not by uncalled-for variations in structure. When attempting to "parallelize" a paragraph, you can remove resulting repetitions by using pronouns and by combining related sentences, not unlike rewriting $3ax + 5ay$ as $a(3x + 5y)$.

How should I punctuate a displayed list?

The rules for punctuating displayed lists vary from book to book (and language to language). Whichever you decide to apply, be consistent. For written documents, consistency suggests using in lists the general rules of punctuation and capitalization: thus, capitals and periods for full sentences, and commas or semicolons to separate phrases or clauses within a sentence. For oral presentations, the desire to be visual may suggest dropping the punctuation marks in lists (and perhaps in some other text items).

Common not only in written documents but also on oral presentation slides, lists too often exhibit shortcomings that render them plainly ineffective. Lists are for displaying comparable items in a way that encourages their comparison or memorization, not for making a loose set of items look organized. Whether they are displayed (with or without bullets) or typeset as part of a solid paragraph, lists should

- comprise few items (in other words, five or fewer), to allow their nonsequential, visual processing;

- introduce the items by a clause (or part of one), to let the readers know what the list is about;

- phrase all items in a grammatically similar way, to reflect in the form the parallelism of content.

The manner in which the items are phrased should obviously be a grammatically correct continuation of the introductory component. The use of bullets to reveal items does not alter the rules of grammar.

- To prepare a meeting, define its purpose
- You must also prepare an agenda
- Everyone should receive this agenda
- Does everyone know who the others are?
- The chairperson should not be secretary
- Ground rules may be appropriate, too
- Always review the purpose and agenda

When preparing a meeting,
- define the purpose and agenda,
- send the agenda to all participants.

As you start the meeting,
- welcome and introduce participants,
- clarify the roles (chair, secretary, etc.),
- set up ground rules if appropriate,
- review the purpose and the agenda.

parallel link

The nozzle includes a scatterer. It is easy to mount.

The nozzle includes a scatterer. This scatterer is …

serial link

Recent years have seen an increased popularity of codes based on the Diabolo algorithm. Speed is a main advantage of these codes, compared to the traditional Demon ones. Also, one can implement them reasonably easily, and it is possible to extend them so they can handle hybrid transforms. On the other hand, they require about 45% more memory, but this is less critical with today's architectures. Typical applications are …

All current implementations of the Diabolo algorithm are based on the so-called Angel transform. F. Angel first described this transform in [2]. The idea is to separate the data into high and low values before proceeding with generation. The implementation then stores the high and low values separately …

Above all else, sentences within a paragraph are connected by content: one element in a sentence, normally its subject, points to an element in the previous sentence. A reference to the previous subject is best done with a personal pronoun (*it*, *they*, *we*, etc.), whereas a reference to the previous object or other item appearing at the end of the previous sentence is best indicated by a demonstrative adjective (*this*, *such*, etc.). By analogy with elementary electrical circuits, we might call the first case a parallel link and the second case a serial link.

Parallel or serial links can be repeated for several sentences: a parallel structure lines up sentences with the same subject,

> In recent years, codes based on the Diabolo algorithm have become increasingly popular. Compared to the traditional Demon codes, they are about twice as fast, are reasonably easy to implement, and can be extended to handle hybrid transforms. As a drawback, they require about 45% more memory, a less critical limitation with today's architectures. Typically, they are applied to …

whereas a serial structure chains sentences by using what is introduced in one sentence as the subject of the next sentence.

> All current implementations of the Diabolo algorithm are based on the so-called Angel transform. This transform, first described by F. Angel [2], separates the data into high and low values before proceeding with generation. The high and low values are then stored separately …

Both structures can be used to construct entire paragraphs. The parallel structure, using the paragraph's topic as subject of all its sentences, is the more readily applicable of the two. The serial structure is well suited to introductory paragraphs, organized from general to particular, and to substructures, for example within a more complex parallel–serial paragraph.

I have been told to write in the active voice. How can I then use the topic as the subject?

Do not confuse *active voice* and *first person*. The subject of a verb in the active voice need not be a person; it can be an inanimate object, as in *This paper presents* or *The results show*. Even if you choose to write in the first person, the topic is largely expressed in the verb, too. If you write *we decided*, readers will understand that the sentence is about a *decision* you made, although this word is not the sentence's subject. If all the sentences use *we* as subject, however, readers may feel you are talking about yourself.

I can recognize instances of main information in a subordinate clause, but how can I fix them?

To improve an instance of main information in a subordinate clause, proceed in two steps, as follows. First of all, delete the main clause, so the subordinate clause is now the main one. Then, identify what you have lost, if anything, and add it back, keeping your new main clause.

As an example, if your original sentence reads *Figure 3 shows that the simulation worked well*, first delete *Figure 3 shows that*: your sentence now simply reads *The simulation worked well*. You have, however, lost the link with Figure 3; just put it back, either as a subordinate clause (*As Figure 3 shows, ...*) or simply in parentheses at the end: *The simulation worked well (Fig. 3)*.

In contrast, if your sentence is something like *It was observed that the simulation worked well*, you lose little by deleting *It was observed that*. Quite on the contrary, the simpler statement *The simulation worked well* has more impact, especially as the first sentence of a paragraph.

Common shortcomings

To avoid a passive voice, authors may end up using a subject that is in fact not the paragraph's topic.

> Table 5 summarizes the results of our tests. These results show the superiority of ...

> The results of our tests are summarized in Table 5. They show the superiority of ...

or better, with the details in a subordinate clause,

> The results of our tests, summarized in Table 5, show the superiority of ...

Focused on their work, scientists too often describe an observed phenomenon in a subordinate clause and state in the main clause that it was observed.

> Figure 2 shows that, in most experiments, the rate was lower at higher temperature.

> In most experiments, the rate was lower at higher temperature (Figure 2).

Impersonal main clauses of the form *it is ... that ...* also relegate the message to a subordinate clause, weakening the point they try to draw attention to.

It is clear that ...	Clearly, ...
It is obvious that ...	Obviously, ...
It is a surprise to us that ...	Surprisingly, ...
It can be concluded that ...	In conclusion, ...

Expressing ideas

Sentences are for conveying ideas. Well-constructed sentences, therefore, stem from well-constructed ideas or, conversely, suggest clear and accurate ideas to the readers. Effective sentences reveal the structure and sequence of ideas logically, yet without taxing the readers' short-term memory.

With each sentence, strive to convey one idea and one only. How long the sentence should be thus depends on the idea expressed. Simple ideas can be conveyed in simple sentences consisting of an independent clause; complex ideas require complex sentences, then consisting of a main clause and one or more subordinate clauses. What constitutes a single idea is of course a view of the mind. As recommended for sections and paragraphs, an optimal division into single ideas strikes a balance between few long sentences and many short ones.

A sentence (or a clause) consists of a subject and a predicate, that is, a verb phrase asserting something about the subject. Because subject and verb are central in conveying meaning, they should be selected with care. As a rule, use the "subject" of the expressed idea as grammatical subject of the sentence. If all sentences in a paragraph cover the same topic, this topic can consistently be the subject, yielding a parallel structure.

When writing complex sentences, state the main information in the main clause and relegate the subordinate information to subordinate clauses. Such sentences prioritize the ideas, giving maximum impact to what is most important. They can effectively address mixed audiences, by placing the *new to all* in the main clause and the *new to some* in a subordinate one.

We agreed last week that I would contact Van Belle & Partners about VAT consolidation between ABC and Choc Export. I just did. They believe that the criteria set forth in the April decree for constituting a VAT group are satisfied by these two companies. This means that we can now move forward with …

As we agreed last week, I contacted Van Belle & Partners about VAT consolidation between ABC and Choc Export. In their opinion, these two companies satisfy the criteria set forth in the April decree for constituting a VAT group. Consequently, we can now move forward with the idea …

Is there a maximum length for sentences?

There is no absolute maximum for the length of a sentence, especially when this sentence comprises several clauses: readability stems from structure, not length. The average length of sentences is nonetheless best harmonized with that of paragraphs, to avoid an imbalance.

In languages that locate the verb, or part of it, at the end of a clause, the length of this clause is a direct measure of distance between subject and verb, and should then be kept reasonable.

How can I fix an overly long subject, while keeping it in subject position?

Admittedly, turning a sentence around makes the subject become the object, so it may well shift the sentence's focus in an unwanted way. As an alternative, especially for long subjects that are lists of items, try a forward reference. Instead of writing *..., ..., and ... were carried out*, put the list beyond the sentence (after a colon), and simply replace it by a phrase pointing to it, as in *The following three tasks were carried out.*

Should I rely on readability formulas?

Formulas assessing the readability of a piece of text on the basis of its average word length, average sentence length, and similar measures have little applicability to educated audiences. Most were developed for school-age children reading in English as their first language, hence they must be extrapolated with caution, if at all. For example, educated non-native speakers are often more familiar with long technical terms than with short words having several meanings.

A long subject with a short predicate may be logical, but it is difficult to process. It is a common issue with tasks or objects expressed in the passive voice.

A finite-element simulation of the principal component's critical subparts was performed.

We performed a finite-element simulation of the principal component's critical subparts.

Equally difficult to process is a new item positioned before an item that refers to the previous sentence.

.... Chapter 4 of the *Safety handbook for the laboratory* discusses this issue.

.... This issue is discussed in Chapter 4 of the *Safety handbook for the laboratory*.

Finally, long parenthetical information in the middle of a sentence is best relocated at the very end of it.

Two hours later, a standard breakfast, consisting of 4 slices of buttered bread, 1 slice of cheese, 1 slice of ham, jelly, and 2 cups of coffee or tea, was served to the subjects.

Two hours later, the subjects were served a standard breakfast, consisting of four slices of buttered bread, a slice of cheese, a slice of ham, jelly, and two cups of coffee or tea.

Although logically constructed, some sentences prove hard to read because they strain the readers' short-term memory. When two related sentence parts, such as a subject and a verb, are far away from each other, readers must store the first part in their short-term memory (not knowing what to do with it) while processing the sentence further; only when they reach the second part can they attribute meaning to the two together. A similar difficulty arises when the two related sentence parts are close to each other, but the first one happens to be long.

What makes a sentence hard to read, then, is the necessity to store items before they can acquire meaning. In contrast, sentence length, frequently decried as hindering readability, is but a symptom: the longer the sentence, the higher the risk of taxing the short-term memory of the readers. Short or long, however, sentences with two or more levels of nested clauses will likely be hard to read. In contrast, carefully constructed long sentences can be almost as easy to read as short ones, while conveying relationships that short sentences could not.

In other words, look out for distance issues in your writing: keep together what goes together, within and across sentences, and place short items before long ones as much as possible. Moreover, to help readers figure out quickly how a sentence relates to previous ones (so they need not store it to do so), show links with connection words: conjunctions, adverbs, etc.

Some information is intrinsically hard to convey in a sentence, no matter how well written. It might then be better conveyed more visually, for example as a formula, a table, or a diagram.

Dick, who, when Jane arrived, left, returns.

Although short, the above sentence is hard to read because of its embedded structure (a subordinate clause within another one).

The sensors were built on a silicon substrate prepared with 370 nm SiO_2 and 160 nm Si_3N_4, and consist of a 215-nm–thick Ti/Pt heating element, 165-nm-thick TiW/Au electric contacts, and a 286-nm-thick SnO_x gas-sensitive layer.

The sensors were built on a silicon substrate made of SiO_2 (370 nm) and Si_3N_4 (160 nm). They consist of three layers:

a heating element	Ti/Pt	215 nm
a set of electric contacts	TiW/Au	165 nm
a gas-sensitive layer	SnO_x	286 nm

Is the passive voice always suboptimal?

The passive voice can be effective, for example to use a certain topic as the sentence's subject, as part of a parallel or serial structure. Its use must not be judged in isolation but in context. (Used as a default, however, it is suboptimal.)

Can I write "the authors" instead of "we"?

Writing *the authors* is as accurate as writing *we* (except near a reference call, where it might seem to designate the authors of the document referred to). However, it is not equally concise.

Can I clarify the agent with a reference call?

Writing *It is believed [5]* in an attempt to mean *The authors of [5] believe* remains ambiguous. All the reference call indicates to the readers is that they can find more on this belief in [5].

Are there ineffective uses of the first person?

The first person is best used exclusively to refer to the authors for tasks, decisions, beliefs, etc. If used too often or in reference to other people, it loses impact through dilution. For example, it is unnecessary for objects of the document. Instead of writing *In this chapter, we present*, write about the chapter: *This chapter presents*. Also unnecessary in most documents is a *we* designating the reader and the author together, as in *We see in Equation 4 that* ..., a first person that ends up relegating the main information to a subordinate clause. (Such a collective *we* might be useful in tutorials, but it should then not be mixed with a *we* that means *the authors*.)

In an attempt to sound objective, many documents seem to imply that their authors never do anything. A task as simple as *We analyzed the data* typically sees its agent removed (*The data were analyzed*) and often its action verb nominalized (turned into a noun): *An analysis of the data was carried out*. Authors might have been taught in school, usually without rationale, never to write in the first person, or have figured it out from the documents they read. Powerful cultural influences quickly lead to myths: many authors now regard the first person as taboo.

More than a question of style, the widespread use of the passive voice raises an issue of accuracy— the concern here is the missing agent, not the voice or grammatical person, even if the three are linked. Admittedly, the agent may not matter or might be understood from context; in such cases, however, the outcome likely matters more than the action: *The analysis of the data indicated* .... Often, though, knowing *who did it* makes a difference to readers, so a task almost always requires an explicit agent. As another example, the main clause *It is believed* is ambiguous: it may be interpreted equally well as *The authors believe* or as *The community believes*.

Overuse of the first person unpleasantly suggests that the authors are in fact writing about themselves, not about their topic. As an alternative, authors can focus on outcome, not action, and clarify their role with a first-person subject in a subordinate clause (*The option that we selected is* ...) or a possessive (*Our analysis suggested a new course of action:* ...), in particular as part of a parallel or serial structure. A collective is another option (*The team decided* ...).

In documents having a single author, a first person plural (*we*) not otherwise clarified lacks accuracy (the author and who else?). It is thus best replaced the first time it appears by an explicit expression: *My supervisor and I* or *My department*, for example.

Being clear, accurate, and concise

WORD CHOICE AFFECTS READABILITY: unusual words make a text unclear; uncalled-for passive voices make it inaccurate; wordy expressions make it longer than necessary. Typing or language mistakes are a major source of noise, too.

For clarity, use words with a known, unambiguous meaning for your audience. Thus, for specialists, use technical terms, but avoid jargon. For nonspecialists, prefer common words, used consistently; avoid synonyms. For non-native readers, beware of so-called false friends (*faux amis*) and of words with multiple meanings; avoid idioms and cultural references.

For accuracy, select each sentence's subject and verb carefully. Identify the agent whenever this agent matters to the readers, as with verbs that imply a human judgment or responsibility, such as *decide, believe,* or *recommend.* If you are the agent, consider using a first person. Express the action with a verb, not with a noun. By default, cast this verb in the active voice, even with an inanimate subject (*with this method, the volume is underestimated → this method underestimates the volume*).

For conciseness, use the shortest phrase allowing the desired level of clarity and accuracy. Avoid ineffective redundancies (*fewer in number*), wordy expressions (*in the event that → if*), and nominalizations (*perform an examination of → examine*). Replace frequently used phrases by acronyms, typeset these and these only in capitals, and introduce them systematically. To avoid repetitions, try combining closely related sentences.

The number of triangles that are used to describe a mesh can be scaled up or down. This can be achieved by performing edge collapses and vertex splits, respectively, as shown in Figure 6.

▶

The number of triangles used to describe a mesh can be scaled up or down through edge collapses or vertex splits, respectively (Figure 6).

Conciseness is a second-draft optimization. On a first draft, concentrate on expressing messages clearly and accurately. Then look for opportunities to say the same in fewer words.

Formatting the document

FORMATTING IS ABOUT STRUCTURE, not about aesthetics. An effective page layout conveys the structure visually, as a form of effective redundancy, yet without drawing attention onto itself, lest it create noise. Like careful phrasing, it goes unnoticed: readers take note of content, not of form.

Visual structure is primarily a matter of spatial arrangement (where items are) and secondarily a matter of visual aspect (how items look). Much can be achieved with spacing alone: the margins and the possible indentations, the line spacing, the space between paragraphs or between headings and text, and juxtaposition, clustering, or alignment of items on a page. Type variation, such as a change in face, size, weight, or color, should merely reinforce what is already conveyed by position.

In contrast to text, a page has two dimensions. A page layout can do more than break a text into a vertical sequence of lines: it can use the horizontal dimension of the page, too, to enrich the visual structure and thus provide additional entry points to the readers. For example, a narrower main column of text (as on this page) leaves space for illustrations and other items directly next to the text, thus opening up a second dimension.

Creating a page layout is more than tinkering with a text file. It requires coming up with a global picture of the final page. This picture can be described as a design grid: a set of points, lines, and areas that guide the positioning and dimensioning of all items consistently and harmoniously across the pages.

Aesthetics, of course, does matter—ugliness distracts. Still, it is best regarded as a consequence of effective formatting, not as a purpose in itself. Even beautiful pages should reveal the structure and thus invite the readers to process the texts, not dazzle the readers to the point that they not wish to read. More than beauty, formatted pages should possess elegance, a quality implying appropriateness, simplicity, and harmony.

The grid used for the right pages in this book, showing the column of text (right) and the grid subset for aligning the illustrations (left).

Common shortcomings

Should drafting always precede formatting?

Logically, a text must have been drafted before it can be formatted, so *drafting* appears before *formatting* in the methodology proposed here. Still, the format might pre-exist or be designed before the text is drafted. Layout constraints, as on the length of texts, should be identified early, so the texts can be optimized accordingly.

Should I prefer boldface or italics for emphasis?

Boldface and italics have different properties. One can notice bold words merely by looking at the page, without actually reading any text. As a consequence, boldface should be reserved for that which readers must notice at a glance, that is, almost solely navigational information: headings, "pseudoheadings" such as *Warning* next to a warning (but not the warning itself), and identifiers such as *Figure 4* under a figure (but, again, not the caption itself). Bold words within a sentence make little sense: typically, they cannot be assigned meaning in isolation. Italicized words, by contrast, do not stand out at a glance but still provide enough emphasis to stand out when the sentence is being read.

How can I use color optimally?

Color in page layout is a dangerous temptation: use it whenever it helps convey the structure, not whenever you can. Use it redundantly, too: not everyone distinguishes colors equally well. Unless you master color design, use few colors, perhaps just one (besides black) in a few tints. Design the page in black and white first, then apply color in touches wherever it adds value. Of course, use this color scheme consistently.

As a common violation of the proximity principle, many reports formatted with direct-manipulation text processors show headings as close (or closer) to the previous paragraph as to the next paragraph, probably as a typing error, not as a design choice.

Ideally, any piece of text should be typeset in a way that keeps together what goes together. In practice, however, few can. Among these few are headings on more than one line, which can be cut by hand.

3.2 Implementation in the long term ▶ 3.2 Implementation in the long term

Finally, many documents leave little empty space on the page and thus afford little design freedom. Often, they attempt to make headings prominent by setting them in a much larger or heavier type, which looks cramped between paragraphs of text. In most cases, a heading need not be (much) larger than the body text; instead, it needs enough space.

Designing intuitive page layouts

P AGE LAYOUTS, like all visual displays, should be intuitive: they should use no arbitrary codes; rather, they must rely on natural principles of proximity, similarity, prominence, and visual sequence. An effective layout reveals the structure of a page at a glance, before the readers even start reading.

When designing a page or spread, group related items visually. Leave more distance between unrelated items than between related ones. For example, leave more space above a heading (between the heading and material preceding it) than below it. Display a caption closer to the corresponding figure or table than to other items on the page, such as other figures or tables. Avoid breaking a line of text between tightly connected items, as in cross-references (Figure|9) and values with units (4|km).

To be intuitive, be visually consistent: format identical items identically, similar items similarly, different items differently. For example, format all same-level headings in the same way (same typeface, type size, relative position, etc.). Conversely, format headings at different levels in visibly different ways, not only in the document, but also in the table of contents. Strive for visual consistency within each document separately but also across comparable documents, as within a collection.

To indicate hierarchy, display more prominently those items that rank higher or that are more important. For example, leave more space around the higher-level headings, set them in a larger or heavier type, or combine several such features. Prominence stems from contrast, so beware of visual inflation: the more items you emphasize, the less they will stand out.

Finally, make sure that each page guides the readers visually along a useful reading sequence or, alternatively, that it gives a clear picture of possible entry points. Where will readers likely look first? Why? Is this where you want them to start? Where do you want them to go next? Is the transition clear?

Plain text is most legible

What kind of typeface should I use?

The legibility of text typefaces has more to do with their familiarity than with their features. Select a design that is familiar to the audience or one that is part of your corporate identity. Optimize text legibility by adjusting type size and, accordingly, line length and line spacing.

May I mix several typefaces?

When mixing typefaces, strive for consistency and harmony. Give each face a function, one that will be readily understood by the readers. Beware of creating a visual cacophony, though; when possible, select faces within one family, as these were designed to work well together.

Is there an optimal text width?

As a first approximation, and unless the page design dictates otherwise, make the text width twice the length of a lowercase Latin alphabet set in the chosen typeface at the chosen size. (Narrower text allows a slightly faster reading but requires more line breaks, some of which may hinder readability, defeating the purpose.)

Should I justify text?

Justifying a text results in sharper text blocks but less natural word spacing and line breaks. Advantage and drawback should be balanced. If markedly rectangular paragraphs contribute to a clearer overall page structure, for example because they align nicely with the other items on the page, you may prefer to justify the text. For a less formal look, leave the text unjustified.

To be recognized rapidly, words must look familiar. They are then identified globally, that is, as a whole rather than letter by letter, as evidenced by the fact we can still largely make out sloppy handwriting. Any visual effect modifying a word's overall shape unavoidably renders this word harder to recognize. The five effects below are common shortcomings.

physics

Avoid unusual typefaces, especially for body text. Such faces may help create a desired atmosphere, as for a commercial ad or for a wedding invitation, but they are not designed for legibility. (Of course, what is an unusual face depends on the audience.)

physics

Avoid setting text in uppercase (except acronyms). By giving them a more similar shape, all uppercase makes the words harder to differentiate. Moreover, by suggesting an acronym, it may mislead readers. In e-mail, it is considered the equivalent of shouting.

PHYSICS

Avoid underlining text or crossing the descenders (the part of the letter extending below the baseline). Besides affecting the silhouette of the whole word, underlining renders the individual letters harder to recognize (an underlined *y* resembles a *v*, etc.).

<u>physics</u>

Avoid setting text on top of a background picture or any nonuniform background (a solid color is OK). A background may make the page more attractive, but it always reduces the legibility of overlaid text. Text and illustrations are best set next to each other.

physics

Avoid packing the lines tightly. Tight lines interfere with one another visually. When long, they make it hard for readers to find the start of the next line. For its overall shape to be readily perceived, a word must be surrounded by enough unoccupied space. Accordingly, plan for sufficient margins around text, too, in particular inside a box: let your text breathe.

physics
biology

physics

Achieving simplicity and harmony

Train	Paris	London
9005	06:43	07:58
9007	07:13	08:28
9009	07:43	08:59
9011	08:07	09:34
9015	09:07	10:36
9019	10:13	11:28
9027	12:13	13:28
9031	13:01	14:34
9039	15:13	16:36
9043	16:13	17:34
9047	17:13	18:34
9049	17:43	18:59
9051	18:13	19:34
⋮	⋮	⋮

Train	Paris	London
9005	06:43	07:58
9007	07:13	08:28
9009	07:43	08:59
9011	08:07	09:34
9015	09:07	10:36
9019	10:13	11:28
9027	12:13	13:28
9031	13:01	14:34
9039	15:13	16:36
9043	16:13	17:34
9047	17:13	18:34
9049	17:43	18:59
9051	18:13	19:34
⋮	⋮	⋮

THE SEEMINGLY ENDLESS formatting possibilities offered by software applications are a curse as much as a blessing: used indiscriminately (too often because they are available rather than because they are useful), they introduce noise. In contrast, optimal formats are visually concise: they reveal the structure by adding the least amount of ink to the page. Prevention is better than cure. In visual design, a healthy dose of self-restraint favors simplicity, consistency, and harmony.

Consider developing a first design under strict, self-imposed constraints, on the basis of relative position on the page only, thus using a single typeface at one or perhaps two type sizes, no variation such as boldface or italic, no color besides black. Once this design satisfactorily conveys the structure visually, you can relax any of the constraints when doing so adds value. If you do, carry the change consistently across the document.

When setting text, use typographical devices sparingly, if only to maintain their impact when used; use space above all else. To make a piece of text stand out, just set it apart: increase its distance from other items, thus surrounding it with space. For example, leave enough space above and below headings. For more contrast, consider increasing the type size or weight slightly. To emphasize words within a paragraph, use italics. As a rule, avoid other typesetting effects, such as underlining.

For harmony, coordinate both the dimension and the position of all the items on the page (paragraphs, figures, tables, etc.), for example by adjusting them to an underlying design grid. For languages that read from left to right, prefer left-aligned blocks of text (not necessarily at the left margin of the page) and consider aligning the other items on their left edge, too, perhaps on the same alignment axis as the paragraphs of text.

Finally, remember that the format should work redundantly: structure and emphasis must already be conveyed by the text.

Fundamentals

    The name of the game
    The three laws of communication
    A thousand words, a thousand pictures
    Chains and magical numbers
    Trees, maps, and theorems

Effective written documents

    Planning the document
    Designing the document
    Drafting the document
    Formatting the document
    Revising the document ———————————— Testing the document
                                         Improving the document
                                         Reviewing documents of others

Effective oral presentations

    Planning the presentation
    Designing the presentation
    Creating slides
    Delivering the presentation
    Answering questions

Effective graphical displays

    Understanding pictures
    Planning the graph
    Designing the graph
    Constructing the graph
    Drafting the caption

Applications

    Effective instructions
    Effective electronic mail
    Effective Web sites
    Effective meeting reports
    Effective scientific posters

Revising the document

Planning

Designing

Drafting

Formatting

Revising

Finished
document

DOCUMENTS ARE SELDOM OPTIMAL as a very first draft. Hence they must be revised more or less intensively, according to the required or desired level of quality. While a routine letter may need no more than proofreading by its author, a more important document usually benefits from a second opinion or perhaps from a more formal test.

Key to optimizing the document, revising is an integral part of the writing process, not "something you do if you have time." Accordingly, it must be taken into account in the time budget. It is not a last step as much as a decision to iterate and refine the other steps: drafting, formatting, and if needed designing or even planning. Each step will need all the fewer iterations when the preceding steps have been completed with care: if the planning must be reconsidered, so must, most probably, the designing, the drafting, and the formatting, in that order.

The need to iterate (part of) the writing process always rests on the answer to the question, is the document good enough? Past a certain stage, this question is a difficult one to answer for the authors themselves: how can they assess the clarity of what they have written unless they test it on someone else? Feedback from such test readers is an invaluable contribution to the optimization process: we must treasure it, not fear it.

After testing it in one way or another, we can start improving the document. More than a specific set of skills, this step requires a positive attitude, including the willingness to listen to test readers (even if discerningly), to change the document accordingly, and eventually to proofread everything carefully. Proofreading, a way to filter out noise, should not be neglected, even for such quick documents as short electronic messages.

Finally, knowing what feedback is useful to us should help us provide more useful feedback when we review the documents of others—a more difficult task than it might seem at first.

Common shortcomings

Can I test the document myself?

Testing a document suggests "discovering" it (looking at it and reading it for the first time), so you cannot quite test your own document as someone else can. You can, however, take a fresh look at it by setting it aside for a while. Obviously, the longer you can wait, the better. In any case, let it rest at least a night: sleeping helps you distance yourself from the situation.

Why should I not defend my text when test readers attack it?

What seems like an attack should not be taken as one. For example, a reader who points out *this is unclear* really means *I found this unclear*; this is an incontrovertible statement—arguing back that *this is perfectly clear* makes no sense. Feel free, of course, to think so and to decide not to modify that part of the text, but arguing will only make readers less willing to provide feedback in the future. Moreover, if one reader found a piece of text unclear, so may others. Therefore, finding out what exactly this reader found unclear is a more constructive approach.

What if the test reader is my boss?

Saying that the author has final responsibility on the document is a first approximation only: the author's organization is responsible, too, so disregarding comments you disagree with may be harder when they come from the boss. If you feel you must argue, argue about ideas, not about words. If your supervisor dislikes a phrase and you dislike his or her rewording, see if you disagree on content. If not, search for a third wording that you can both agree on.

Revising one's document is usually a difficult task for everyone: hurried writers regard it as a waste of time; careful writers put much pride in their draft and hence feel an emotional barrier to amending it. As a result, this fifth step is prone to imperfections.

For documents not tested on or reviewed by others, the most common (and most severe) shortcoming is skipping the revising step entirely and regarding as a finished document what is in fact still a draft. This attitude is all too frequent for electronic mail, sent as soon as it is drafted, without even as much as undergoing proofreading. Besides carelessness, a lack of revision may come from a tight deadline, which might be caused by poor time management. Writing at the last minute leaves little time not only to go through several iterations but also to leave the draft aside for a while and take a fresh look at it.

Too often, documents that get tested or reviewed go to the wrong people, typically direct colleagues, who know much about the content and the context. True, these readers can usefully check the accuracy of the content; however, they cannot easily detect more fundamental issues of selection and structure: is it the right content, presented in the right order? Anxious authors tend to tell test readers too much about the document, for example by pointing out expected difficulties to them, thus biasing the test (*I have structured the text in [such and such] way. Is this apparent as you read?*—well, it will be now).

Of course, the most frequent revising shortcoming is a defensive inclination on the part of the authors, who then explain or justify what they have written, instead of listening to what test readers have to say. This understandable but unproductive resistance to change also makes authors reluctant to question their document as a whole and hence to consider making in-depth changes in structure or in writing, instead of quick fixes. Revising requires dedication.

Testing the document

DIFFERENT QUALITIES OF A DOCUMENT (clarity, accuracy, correctness, etc.) are best tested on different audiences. To test the clarity of your document, select nonspecialized, secondary readers, that is, people representative of the least specialized, most secondary among your anticipated readers. To test the accuracy of your document, by contrast, prefer specialists. To improve language correctness, select readers who are proficient in the language of your document—ideally native speakers, though being a native speaker is not enough.

When entrusting a copy of your document to readers for a test, clarify what you expect from them and by when, but refrain from telling them anything that might bias the test. Do say whether you are looking for comments on the form (clarity), on the content (accuracy), or on the language (correctness). Specify whether you prefer high-level feedback (for example, because you are still likely to revise the document in depth) or a more detailed analysis. Agree on a deadline, whether it is dictated by schedule (*This must go out on Tuesday, so I need your feedback by Monday*) or negotiated with the test readers (*By when do you think you can get back to me about this?*).

When receiving your commented copy from the test readers, be receptive, not defensive. Whenever practical, sit together with each test reader to review his or her feedback. Make sure you understand each annotation's meaning and importance. Ask questions on the parts that received few or no comments: the readers may have an opinion that they did not write down. If the "comment" is in fact a rewording, ask what was wrong with the original wording. Should you disagree with a remark or rewording, focus on understanding the reader's viewpoint, not on defending your own. You, as author, can decide later whether to change the sentence as suggested by this reader or to keep it as is. Defending your text defeats the purpose of the test, which is to collect readers' reactions accurately, so you can make informed decisions about what to change.

Can I proofread the document myself?

Proofreading one's own document is difficult. When expecting a certain word in a certain place, one uses in fact very little visual information to recognize the word—too little, most often, to ascertain that the word is spelled correctly. As with testing the document, setting it aside for a while certainly helps. So does changing its visual appearance, such as setting the text in a different typeface, at a different type size, or with a different line spacing or line width.

Should I use a grammar checker?

Grammar checkers are much less reliable than spell-checkers are: they are limited to flagging potential problems on the basis of symptoms and letting the author decide whether there is indeed a grammatical error and how to fix it. While they may be useful to those who master the language, they tend to be confusing, if not downright misleading, for non-native writers, who may be unable to recognize false alarms and who thus tend to trust the checker blindly.

Why should I proofread a manuscript I submit to a journal? Surely they have a proofreader.

Texts that will be further edited, as is usually the case for scientific papers being submitted to a journal, will most likely be proofread later by a qualified person. If the article must first be refereed, however, errors might needlessly antagonize the referees and also prevent them from paying due attention to your messages. Polished documents always reflect positively on the authors and, indirectly, on their work. Careless documents suggest careless research.

Having a skilled editor improve our documents is certainly comfortable but not necessarily optimal. Such an editor is unlikely to know as well as we do what messages or ideas we are trying to get across. If we hand him or her an unpolished draft (which is tempting when we know it will still be improved), we risk misunderstandings and inappropriate edits. Moreover, and unless we take time with the editor to review the changes and the reasons behind them, we will not learn much from the editing process and thus not improve our writing for the situations for which we will not have the luxury of an editor.

A way to systematize how we improve documents and to sharpen our writing skills by the same token is to maintain a list of the errors we tend to make, as identified in the feedback we collect from others. We can then look for each of these errors in turn, using the search capabilities of our text processor. Such a search typically helps us identify in isolation errors we understand but nonetheless overlooked. If we tend to write *insure* when we mean *ensure*, for example, we can search for instances of *insure* and verify whether they are what we meant to write. This process will not only improve our documents but also help automatize the correct use of the term: after a while, the documents we write will probably no longer contain any instance of a misused *insure*.

Besides misused words, easy-to-search-for errors include the following ones: inaccurate expressions such as *a number of* (to be replaced by the number), verbose expressions such as *at this point in time* to mean *now*, misspellings that pass spell-checkers such as *it's* instead of *its*, false friends such as *actual*, having a different meaning in English and Spanish, and consistency of terminology, such as choosing between *user guide*, *user's guide*, and *user manual*. With some ingenuity, you can even devise patterns to search for suboptimal sentences as with *it must be pointed out that*, *was carried out*, or *is believed*.

Improving the document

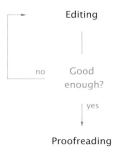

Editing

no   Good
       enough?

       | yes

Proofreading

I MPROVING A DOCUMENT proceeds in two steps: editing it iteratively, among other things on the basis of the feedback provided by the test readers; then, proofreading it carefully. The first step suggests looking for ways to improve further what is still unfinished work. In contrast, the second means inspecting what is otherwise considered a finished document. While editing is normally an activity for the authors, if only for a consistent style, proofreading can be entrusted to others.

When editing a written document, make major changes first and minor ones afterwards. Indeed, major changes may well get rid of minor problems, whereas the reverse is seldom true. To identify possible major changes, work on a paper printout, not at your computer screen. Printed pages provide not only a better overview of the document but also a flexible medium for fast marking, such as crossing out words or sentences, indicating moves with arrows, or making notes in the margin. Text processors on computer screens, in contrast, encourage local revisions in the phrasing and the formatting of the text.

After editing the document iteratively until it seems optimal, proofread it in several passes. In each pass, check one aspect of the document: content (such as numerical data), spelling, formatting, cross-references, etc. Remember to proofread not only the full paragraphs but also the isolated text items, such as headings or captions. Use any means available to you, such as a checklist, a spell-checker, or help from colleagues, but do not trust technology blindly: there are spelling errors that a spell-checker, however smart, will be unable to spot.

What fraction of a writing project's time budget should be reserved for editing and proofreading is difficult to determine: it depends of course on the quality of the draft to be revised. Anyway, it should not be underestimated: it may take as long, if not several times as long, as developing a solid first draft, depending on the quality level required of the final document.

Common shortcomings

How can I clarify different types of feedback?

Colors may help qualify feedback. Still, black and blue, while neutral, typically lack contrast with the printed text. Red is better contrasted but often connotes error or perhaps judgment and might then needlessly antagonize authors; green is usually a less threatening alternative. As a useful color scheme, you might thus use red for language errors or mandatory changes, green for suggested changes, and black pencil (perhaps with text highlighter) for comments.

Some authors are defensive or easily offended. How can I provide tactful feedback to them?

Strive not to seem threatening or judgmental: show that your comments are meant to help. To suggest that you are "on the authors' side," try phrasing suggestions with a *we*, not a *you*. For example, instead of writing *Could you turn this passive voice into an active one?*, consider writing *Could we turn ....* Similarly, and to avoid antagonizing authors who do not take orders, try pointing out possible issues as a question, not as a statement (or, worse, as a command). When spotting an apparent lack of consistency, for example, instead of ordering *Be consistent*, you may ask them, *Is the difference intentional?* They probably prefer to conclude themselves as to the inconsistency than to be told by you.

Is reviewing the same as refereeing?

Refereeing an article implies a judgment about whether to accept it for publication in a journal. It thus involves more than reviewing the article. Referees ascertain its suitability for the journal and—ideally—also help its author(s) improve it.

To contribute effectively to improving a document and, ideally, to help authors become better writers, reviewers must do more than indicate corrections: they must strive to provide tactful, helpful feedback, that is, feedback that will be accepted by authors and from which authors can draw valuable lessons. An oral discussion helps get a constructive attitude across, but it is not always practical. In any case, oral feedback typically builds on written feedback, so this feedback should be phrased most carefully.

Reviewers, unfortunately, easily confuse reviewing with rewriting, much to the frustration of authors. Unless they have a poor command of the language, authors indeed expect comments about their text, not replacement text, which they feel is not theirs. When they see a sentence crossed out and replaced by another, they are left to think, *what was wrong with my original sentence?* They expect reviewers to point out any issues rather than offer solutions to unidentified problems. (As it happens, however, reviewers often feel something is wrong but lack the analytical framework to put the issue in words.)

When they leave it to authors to correct a problem, reviewers are sometimes unclear in their comments. Many authors have been puzzled by a squiggly line next to a paragraph, without further clarification— or with a question mark or a vague *To be rewritten*. Authors can rewrite the paragraph a dozen times, but how could they improve it if they are not told what exactly the reviewer finds suboptimal about it?

How blunt reviewers can be in providing feedback depends largely on national and corporate culture. Still, three types of criticism are needlessly negative: judgment (*this sounds silly*), reproach (*you should have used the active voice here*), and interpretation (*obviously, you are trying to bluff your audience*). They are best replaced by constructive alternatives, more likely to elicit learning, no matter the culture.

Reviewing documents of others

REVIEWING A DOCUMENT so as to provide helpful feedback to its authors is no easy task. It requires careful reading to identify problematic passages, sharp analytical thinking to pinpoint the exact shortcoming in each of these passages, and a fair amount of tact to communicate these shortcomings to the authors in a constructive way, for an optimal process.

As usual, refrain from rushing into the task at hand: plan first. When you are requested to review someone else's document, agree on the deliverable: make sure both you and the authors or review coordinator are clear on the type of review needed, the state of the document (partial or complete, draft level), and the deadline. Next, choose an appropriate place and time, and arrange not to be disturbed during a long enough period. As for revising your own text, work preferably on a paper copy.

When reviewing the document, center yourself on the purpose that was agreed upon, such as clarity, accuracy, or correctness. Should this purpose be multiple, review one aspect at a time, focusing on content first. Typos are usually more conspicuous than reasoning flaws but also less important. When reviewing for content, try to ignore any other potential sources of noise.

In your comments to the authors, strive to help, not to judge. First, provide a global assessment, to place further comments in proper perspective. As a rule, point out the weaknesses, to prompt improvements, but also the strengths, to increase the authors' willingness to revise the document and to learn. Make comments explicit in both their object and their nature: content versus form, incorrect use versus inelegant wording, and (if you have authority over the authors) required changes versus mere suggestions. Moreover, and whenever practical, consider an oral discussion to clarify your written comments and, if needed, to look with the authors for suitable solutions. As a last step, make sure everyone is clear on what to do next with the document (revision, second review, approval, etc.).

*Le secret d'ennuyer
est de vouloir tout dire.*

— Voltaire

*It usually takes me more than three weeks
to prepare a good impromptu speech.*

— Mark Twain

Effective oral presentations

ORAL PRESENTATIONS are about having something to say to one's audience and being able to say it in an articulate way while looking them in the eye. They are about engaging the audience with mind and body, conveying well-structured messages with sincerity, confidence, and, yes, passion. They are about presence, about being seen and being heard, not about having the audience look at slides that are in fact written pages, while hoping not to be noticed.

An effective way to go from scratch to a finished presentation proceeds in five steps, not unlike for documents. First, plan the presentation: gather your thoughts about the occasion. Second, design it: organize your content into a simple outline. Third, create the slides that will help convey your messages. Fourth, rehearse the presentation until you feel confident, and deliver it to your audience. Finally, answer the questions, to clarify or complement the material you have just presented.

Planning the presentation

PLANNING AN ORAL PRESENTATION proceeds much like for a written document. We must distance ourselves from the situation and find answers to the questions *why*, *who*, *what*, *when*, and *where*. These questions may have a somewhat different slant for an oral presentation, however.

The purpose (*why*) focuses again on the audience. It identifies, not what the speaker should achieve, but what the listeners should (be able to) do as a result of attending the presentation. The desired action can often be requested explicitly from them, for example in a call for action at the end of the presentation.

The audience (*who*) is better defined for an oral presentation than for a written document: it consists of the attendees only, at least in first approximation. Like the readers of a document, these attendees can be more or less familiar with the content and with the context. Unlike future readers of a document, they can usually be assumed to listen *now* and, to a point, *here*.

The oral defense of a doctoral thesis is, no doubt, the prototype of those situations in which only part of the audience matters for the purpose: the jury, usually composed of specialists. Doctoral students should focus on them more than on nonspecialist family or friends who came to show moral support.

Project proposals, in contrast, must often convince not only the specialists (that the project is sound technically) but also the nonspecialist executives (that the project is worthwhile for the organization).

The content (*what*) should, again, be limited to what serves the purpose and be organized in a way that suits the audience. Be more selective than for a document, though, for listeners cannot be: everyone hears everything. For a mixed audience of specialists and nonspecialists, focus on those who matter for your purpose. If all matter, have something for everyone: use technical terms, but paraphrase them for nonspecialists. If time is short, focus on nonspecialists, but save enough time for specialists to ask questions: as with a written document, in a sense, provide the global view and let them select details.

The speaking situation (*when* and *where*) provides constraints of time and space. Time involves moment (not only what day but also what time of day) and maximum duration (how long). Space regards not only the assigned speaking room but also the setup of this room for the presentation. Both should be investigated ahead of time and, when possible, be optimized.

Designing the presentation

ORAL PRESENTATIONS are intrinsically synchronous. In contrast to written documents, they thus impose both the sequence and the rhythm of presentation: listeners cannot skim or skip parts, listen to the last part first, or go back and listen again to more difficult parts. Moreover, they have fewer visual clues about the structure than readers: unless the speaker clarifies it, they cannot see, for example, that they are starting a new point or are almost at the end.

Oral presentations, on the other hand, allow a richer rapport with the audience, thanks to the very presence of the speaker and the ensuing nonverbal communication (vocal and visual). There is something about face-to-face contact that can never be found in a written document, no matter how well written.

The easiest way to make enemies with the audience is to speak longer than the time they allocate you. Yet predicting a presentation's length is not trivial: many conference speakers are still in the middle of their 15-minute talk when the chair announces *two minutes left*—at which point they simply go on with their planned content, speaking much faster. It is prudent to know what to drop, if short on time. A top-down approach (below) helps set priorities.

Oral presentations, as a consequence, benefit from following a slightly different design strategy than written documents. Whereas documents support messages with detailed evidence, presentations support messages with a convincing delivery, together with sound but usually less detailed argumentation. Because listeners cannot be selective about what they hear, speakers should be. Many speakers just try to say too much; details—if any—are best provided in a companion document.

Oral presentations normally convey one main message only: the sentence that the speaker wants the listeners to remember, were they to remember only one. It should be expressed early in the presentation but also identified early in the design step, for it affects the selection of content. This top-down approach helps prepare a focused presentation, no matter its duration: longer presentations then go further in depth, not in breadth.

Main message What you
want your audience
to remember

Main points
What supports
this message

Subpoints

Oral presentations should also offer clues to their structure, which is otherwise hardly visible. They should provide a map, let the audience know regularly where they are on this map, and summarize the material as a form of effective redundancy.

Customary yet ineffective formulas

How long should the opening be?

The opening of a presentation should be kept
brief, yet elaborate enough to reach its purpose.
Too long an opening will confuse the audience
rather than prepare them for the presentation;
too short an opening will fail to motivate them.
Should the need or task be technically complex,
provide a high-level version only in the opening
and elaborate upon it as you see fit in the body.
In absolute terms, then, an opening might be
as short as 90 seconds for a six-minute speech
and as long as six minutes for a presentation
lasting an hour, but it depends on many factors.

Where should I insert acknowledgments?

Important as they are for those acknowledged,
acknowledgments are of very limited interest
to the rest of the audience and thus hard to fit
without breaking the flow of the presentation.
You can mention your coauthors' contribution,
if sufficiently different from your own, as part
of the task, when you identify "who did what."
You might acknowledge others one at a time,
whenever relevant in your body, or together
at the end. To avoid an anticlimax, you might
do so in a slide you show without comments
after the applause, while answering questions.

*My conclusion is negative. If I state it upfront,
will my audience not lose interest and leave?*

If your negative conclusion comes as a surprise
at the end (*... but unfortunately, it did not work*),
the audience will feel cheated, which is worse.
To keep them interested from the start, focus,
not on what failed, but on what can be gained
(*We can learn valuable lessons from this project*).

The very first and very last words of a presentation
condition the first and last impression the speaker
makes on the audience and must thus be chosen
with care. The customary formulas may not bother
listeners but are not likely to impress them either.
Below are common yet ineffective opening phrases.

> *Well, good afternoon, ladies and gentlemen*
> or similar conventional salutation, spoiling
> the effect of a subsequent attention getter.

> *This afternoon, I'd like to tell you about ...*,
> expressing why the speaker wants to speak,
> not why the listeners might want to listen.

> *In this talk, I'm going to convince you of ...*,
> antagonizing from the start those listeners
> who feel they should decide for themselves.

The last words, often overlooked in the preparation,
resort to various common yet weak formulas, too.

> *So... I guess that's all I have for you today*,
> implying that the speaker ran out of things
> to say, as opposed to closing deliberately.

> *Thank you for your attention*, suggesting
> that the audience paid attention as a favor,
> rather than out of interest in the material.

> *Any questions?* or similar utterance, leaving
> no opportunity for the audience to applaud
> before moving on to questions and answers.

To arouse applause is not an objective in itself, but
a collective manifestation of appreciation reflects
positively on the impression that everyone keeps,
besides being an enjoyable reward for the speaker.
In formal situations, an effective close will normally
trigger applause; wait until the applause subsides
before encouraging the audience to ask questions.

Structuring the content

ORAL PRESENTATIONS CAN BE THOUGHT OF as comprising three distinct parts: an opening, a body, and a closing. The opening, not unlike the abstract of a written document, rapidly presents first the motivation, then the main message. Thus, it states the need for the work reported, as a difference between the actual and desired situations, and then the task, that is, what the speaker had decided or been asked to do to address the need. The body then presents, not all details of the work, but selected evidence in support of the message, structured hierarchically. The closing gives the conclusion, restating—and usually elaborating upon—the main message.

Attention getter
Need
Task
Main message

Point 1

Point 2

⋮

Conclusion
Close

Oral presentations, moreover, can gain considerable impact by starting and ending forcefully, as opposed to hesitantly. Before it can hope to get motivation or main message across, the opening must first attract the attention of the audience, as with a usually unexpected but always relevant statement, question, anecdote, or analogy, leading smoothly to the need. This *attention getter* is the very first impression the speaker makes on the audience, so it must be prepared most carefully. Similarly, the closing should let the audience know in a clear and elegant way that the presentation has come to an end, typically by a change of tone. Such a *close* can simply tie back to the attention getter, to show that the loop has been looped. If appropriate, it can also usefully call the audience to action, as a direct way to increase the chance of reaching the purpose. Attention getter and close should be the first and last words, respectively. Anything said right before the attention getter or right after the close defeats the purpose of these two items.

The opening thus lets the audience know who the speaker is and what he or she is going to talk about, but not without first obtaining the full attention of everyone. Opening sentences such as *Hello, my name is … and I am going to talk about …* fail to appeal to the audience, because they lack motivation. The listeners first want to know why they should listen at all.

Getting off to a good start

What exactly is the difference between need and attention getter? Both of them attempt to get the audience interested, do they not?

The attention getter and need admittedly work hand in hand, but attention is not motivation. An effective attention getter gets the audience to pay attention at once, but for just a moment. An effective need uses this moment to secure their interest in the topic itself, so as to ensure they pay attention to the whole presentation.

How sophisticated must the attention getter be?

Attention getters should serve their purpose: they should be catchy enough to start forcefully and also to establish rapport with the audience, yet they should not be overdramatic, seem out of tone, or pursue originality for its own sake. An informed audience already made attentive by the chair might indeed need no more than *As you probably know, ...* to be lead directly into the need. Many audiences, however, need a stronger beginning to start listening at once.

How about telling a joke as an attention getter?

Stories told solely to arouse laughter are risky. When unsuccessful, they embarrass everyone. And even if they do make the audience laugh, they easily seem irrelevant or out of place. They call attention to the speaker, not to the topic.

If you think humor is in order, be humorous with relevant material. If the audience laugh, so much the better; but even if they fail to find your explanation funny, they will learn from it as from other material. Unless you tell them, they will not know you meant it as humorous.

As the saying goes, you never get a second chance to make a first impression. Thus your opening and, especially, your first few words, play a crucial role. Make sure that these first words are meaningful—not filler words and probably not even customary yet often unnecessary (and always uninteresting) courtesies such as *Well, good afternoon, everyone.*

An attention getter is so much more than a device to obtain silence (this is taken care of by the chair, usually). It is a way to bring the audience from 0% to 100% attentiveness in as little time as possible, leaving as much time as possible for the remainder of the presentation. It is a way to bridge the gap between what the audience may have on their minds and what the speaker is about to discuss, starting with the need. Clearly, it must focus on the audience. So must the need, so as to get the audience to care.

Saying your name and the title of your presentation, as many speakers do, is usually an ineffective start: it focuses on you and your topic, not your audience. This audience cares little about your name just yet, for they do not know what you have done for them. As for the title of your talk, it is written language, meant to be read, not said. Put it on a title slide (with your name), but do not feel obliged to say it.

From your first words, then, focus on introducing your audience to your content. Get their attention with something they can relate to, often unexpected but always relevant. With their attention on what leads into the topic, make them care with a need. Then—and only then—put yourself in the picture by showing in a task how you have done something to address this need that the audience cares about. This task is the right place to clarify who you are. More than saying your name (already mentioned by the chair or shown on your title slide), establish your connection with the audience or your expertise in the topic, as with your function, experience, etc.

Below is what the opening of a short presentation in a reasonably informal setting might sound like. The speaker reports on work done with a colleague to a limited audience of engineers and managers from the teams involved (all familiar with the QNFLP, including its strategic importance, and with BLTs). If this audience is already well aware of the issue, then the first attention getter may sound overdone and the simpler alternative one will likely suffice.

Attention getter—strives to draw everyone's attention to the topic as rapidly as possible by relating this topic to their own concerns.

Imagine what would happen if some of our BLTs gave erroneous results. We can live with one or two of them malfunctioning, of course, but what about 10% of them? The QNFLP would be totally useless. You think it can't happen? Think again. Recently, …

or alternatively

As you know, the development of the QNFLP relies critically on the correct functioning of the 64 BLTs at each of the 20 locations. Recently, however, …

Need—motivates the audience by telling (or by reminding) them why something had to be done; closes in on a specific problem.

… the Readout Assembly team noticed that some of the BLTs they had inserted in the readout chain behaved incorrectly. They think it is about 1 in 10. They reported this to the people in the BLT team, who test every BLT before it goes out to assembly, but these BLT people did not observe the problem.

Task—identifies "who did what" in an effort to address the need; situates the speaker with respect to the audience and to the topic.

So Luis Primo, the head of the BLT team, asked us in R&D to investigate this mystery, and Jacqueline Keely, in charge of the R&D department, assigned the study to Wonga Aries, here, and myself, given our past work on the PBJ—the precursor of the BLT. Wonga and I analyzed the working of various BLTs both in isolation and as part of the readout chain.

Main message—states the main conclusion upfront; also known as *thesis* or *take-home message*.

We believe the malfunction of some BLTs is caused by a thin oxide layer that develops on their contacts in the interval between manufacture and assembly.

Preview—announces the body's content, suggesting how it helps support or develop the message just stated; also known as *outline*.

What makes us think so and, especially, what can we do about it? Well, let us look first of all at what folks in Readout Assembly have observed exactly; then let's review the tests Wonga and I conducted and what we can learn from them; as a final step, we can explore solutions to the oxidation problem.

How detailed should the preview be?

The preview should be limited to the top level, that is, two to five points, no matter how long the presentation is. If useful, subpoints can be previewed at the beginning of each main point. A longer presentation includes more material per main point or subpoint, but normally not more subpoints—nor necessarily more slides (one per subpoint)—so the presentation length does not affect the number of items previewed.

Should I show my preview slide again during transitions?

Showing the preview slide each time takes time. For short presentations, it is seldom justified: a shorter spoken transition normally suffices. For long presentations, it is more appropriate, as the audience may have forgotten the map. Rather than showing the exact same preview, prepare a different slide for each transition, highlighting the next main point on the map. On this slide, and if appropriate, you might also preview the subpoints of this next main point.

My speaking time is already so limited. Do I really need to include a review?

Reviews are too often sacrificed for lack of time (or for appearing unnecessary to the speaker), yet they help so much get the message across in a convincing and lasting way. Without one, the audience is unlikely to remember the body of the presentation, at least in a structured way, even if they have understood every part of it. By putting all the pieces of the puzzle together, the review also makes the conclusion sound inescapable, further convincing the audience.

An oral presentation too often leaves the audience with an uncomfortable sensation of disorientation. Even when they enjoyed a presentation, listeners are usually hard-pressed to recall the main points made by the speaker—or to say how many of them the speaker made. Perhaps the structure was fine; at any rate, it was not apparent to the audience or at least not memorable. Revealing the structure tends to be hard for speakers, who need no map to find their way through their own presentation.

Most speakers, when they include a preview at all, present it too early—typically within half a minute, after saying hardly more than the title of their talk. Such a preview is wasted: listeners simply cannot assimilate it so early in the presentation, for lack of reference points. They are not ready for details until they hear about the motivation and outcome, in the form of a need, a task, and a main message.

Even if well timed, many previews are just too hard for listeners to remember, either because they list too many points or because they describe each one in too complex a way (typically in too many words). Using a short label for each point, in the preview and in transitions, makes the structure memorable and is all the more useful in the absence of slides.

Novice speakers have a hard time with transitions, which seem to refuse to come to them on the spot. Even with a clear preview, however, the audience will still get lost if they cannot rely on transitions. Like the rest of the presentation, such transitions can and should be prepared and rehearsed carefully.

Often overlooked, the review may not help listeners understand better, but it will help them remember the case developed in the presentation. To this end, it must do more than repeat the body's structure, as announced in the preview: it must summarize the content, too, thus providing an integrated view.

Providing a map and signposts

TO COME ACROSS AS WELL STRUCTURED, a presentation must do more than simply *be* well structured: it must make the structure and the underlying logic of this structure readily apparent to the audience. A careful opening will flow logically enough, especially if short; so will a careful closing. Both, to some extent, are foreseeable. By contrast, the body, with its hierarchical structure, requires a map and signposts, optimally in the form of a preview, transitions, and a review.

The preview, at the end of the opening, prepares the audience for the structure of the body (like the object of the document). Thus it need include neither the previous items in the opening (indeed, the audience need no longer be prepared for them) nor the items in the closing, for a closing is to be expected: the preview is a map of the body, not of the whole presentation.

Transitions both separate and unite the body's main points by clarifying the logic that underpins the body's organization. They show to the audience not only that one point is complete while the next one is about to start but also that these points are logically connected, as they all support the main message. They tell the audience where they currently are on the map. For long presentations, they can usefully remind the audience of the map, too, whether with spoken words or with a slide.

The review, at the beginning of the closing, not only enables the listeners to remember the arguments but also leads them smoothly into the conclusion by recapitulating the material covered in the body. While the preview conveys structure only, the review conveys both content and structure, by restating the body's main points synthetically as it runs over the map.

For best effect, the preview, transitions, and review should be smoothly integrated into the presentation. Ideally, they talk about the topic (*The system has three advantages*), not about the speaker or presentation (*I will present three advantages*).

Attention getter
Need
Task
Main message
Preview

Point 1
Transition
Point 2
Transition

⋮

Review
Conclusion
Close

Fundamentals

    The name of the game
    The three laws of communication
    A thousand words, a thousand pictures
    Chains and magical numbers
    Trees, maps, and theorems

Effective written documents

    Planning the document
    Designing the document
    Drafting the document
    Formatting the document
    Revising the document

Effective oral presentations

    Planning the presentation
    Designing the presentation
    Creating slides ——————————— Designing the slides
    Delivering the presentation   Constructing the slides
    Answering questions   Handling the slides

Effective graphical displays

    Understanding pictures
    Planning the graph
    Designing the graph
    Constructing the graph
    Drafting the caption

Applications

    Effective instructions
    Effective electronic mail
    Effective Web sites
    Effective meeting reports
    Effective scientific posters

Creating slides

For presentations on short notice, many speakers limit preparation to recycling existing slides and making quick and dirty new ones. When their set of slides is ready, they feel they are, too. Are they?

Their time would be better spent planning and designing the talk, then rehearsing it if time allows, and just forgetting about slides. Slides are not a priority; the talk is.

S LIDES ARE FOR CONVEYING MESSAGES—the same ones as the spoken text conveys. For effective redundancy, both slides and spoken text should stand on their own: "deaf" audience members (for example, non-native speakers with poor listening comprehension skills) should thus be able to grasp the speaker's messages by looking at the slides only, whereas "blind" ones (for example, those taking notes) should be able to grasp the messages by listening to the speaker only.

Slides, meant to be redundant, are a choice, not an obligation. A presentation is not a set of slides: it is all about someone having something to say to an audience—slides or no slides. Indeed, a presentation can be most effective without slides, whereas it can hardly be successful if it is not well planned, well designed, and well delivered. And while effective slides enhance a presentation, poor slides severely detract from it by competing with the speaker for the attention of the audience or by reflecting badly on him or her. There is thus no excuse for poor slides: do your slides right... or don't do slides at all.

A major noise source on slides is text, especially a lot of text, for the audience cannot read one text and listen to another at the same time. An effective slide gets the message across (the *so what*, not merely the *what*) globally, almost instantly. There lies the challenge: to express a message unambiguously with as little text as possible. Visual codings being in essence ambiguous, effective slides almost always include some text: the message itself, stated as a short but complete sentence. Besides this text statement, the message should be developed as visually as possible: this development should include only whatever words are necessary for the slide to stand on its own.

Beyond including no superfluous information in their design, slides should include no superfluous ink in their construction. Optimal slides get messages across clearly and accurately with as few graphical features as possible: they are noise-free.

Most slides just include too much text

Should every slide convey a message?

Ideally, every slide indeed conveys a message, especially for a short, intensive presentation. If you decide to show a slide to your audience, surely you are trying to tell something with it.

Should I not include bibliographical references on slides, to show where the data come from?

Full bibliographical references are often noise. Do you expect audience members to read them? If yes, then do not expect them to listen to you. If no, then why do you include the references? References are important information indeed but are best placed in a companion document.

To give credit to someone for the data you show, simply include the person's name together with the year of publication in Harvard citation style, as in "Doumont, 2005"—not the full reference.

How can I display complex information, such as equations or intricate diagrams?

Before you look for solutions, question the need for displaying complex information on slides: typically, such information can be presented more clearly in a companion document instead.

If you must convey the information on a slide after all, provide a global view before moving to the details. For example, identify and label the main "blocks" of your equation or diagram.

$$\nabla \times \mathbf{B} \quad = \quad \mu_0 \mathbf{J} \quad + \quad \mu_0 \epsilon_0 \frac{\partial \mathbf{E}}{\partial t}$$

current term   field term

Audience members know it: most slides out there include too much information (as text or otherwise) for them to even start processing it while listening to the speaker. Strangely, when these same people become speakers, they too create crowded slides. Why so? Three explanations readily come to mind.

First, many speakers create slides for themselves, as a personal memory aid, not for their audience. These slides are often cryptic (not self-explanatory) and text-heavy. Such material may aid the speaker in preparing or even in delivering the presentation, but it should simply not be shown to the audience.

Second, a drive toward efficiency pushes speakers to think their slides must double as written report. Alas, slides designed with such a purpose in mind tend to include too much to be effective as slides, yet probably too little to make a convincing report. In most situations, they fall short of both objectives.

Third, speakers who create their slides in a hurry often use material copied from written documents (paragraphs, spreadsheets, etc.) without adapting it. They know the result is less than perfect but see it as "better than nothing". Inasmuch as they distract, such slides are in reality worse than no slide at all.

The three reasons above must be complemented by two frequent confusions. First, some speakers conclude that, to stand on their own, slides must include pretty much everything they say. Not so: what appears on the slide must be self-explanatory, but not everything said needs to appear on a slide. Second, and for fear of stating facts out of context, speakers sometimes include extra data on the slide; for example, they mention three numbers but show a detailed table, to allow comparisons if desired. The audience cannot (and should not) spend time analyzing a large table while listening to a speaker, however; such a large table belongs in a handout.

Designing the slides

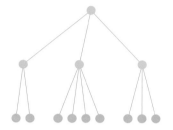

Main message

Main points

Subpoints

Convey each subpoint with a slide

AFTER YOU HAVE STRUCTURED the body of the presentation in main points and subpoints, get each subpoint across with one slide—and one only, at least in first approximation. State the subpoint's message on the slide as a short sentence (in the title area): express the *so what*, not merely the *what*. Illustrate your message as visually as possible, limiting text. Question the pertinence of any item you intend to include; if you are not going to mention it, do not put it on your slide.

A draft by hand may save you many iterations at the computer and help you identify what you need instead of trying to use what you have. First state each of your messages as a sentence and sketch an illustration for it, and later construct all slides.

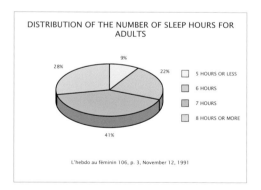

The slide above is poorly designed. First, it conveys no message: the title expresses what the data are, not what the data mean (the *what*, not the *so what*). Second, it is not as visual as it seems: the legend of the pie chart is an arbitrary dictionary of colors, hard to process while one listens to a spoken text. Finally, it is noisy: the pie chart's third dimension distorts the perception of the data, the reference at the bottom will either distract or not be read, etc.

To verify whether your slides stand on their own, show them to someone representative of your audience without providing your spoken text. This someone should be able to figure out *what* each slide displays and *why* you are showing the slide as part of your presentation. Printing the slides in small size (typically six on a page) allows you to test their legibility, too: whatever is hard for you to make out on such a printed page will likely be hard for an audience to make out on the screen.

Should I use a dark background with light text or a light background with dark text?

Ideally, the background of the slides is in tune with the brightness of the room. Historically, the slide projectors and early video projectors required darkness, thus prompting a tradition of slides with a black or dark blue background. Nowadays, projectors are brighter and rooms have lights on, so light backgrounds are better. A white background, as is usual in documents, is most compatible with imported illustrations (and with printing), but backgrounds of a light, solid color (no gradients) have their uses, too.

What kind of typeface should I use on slides?

On (projected) computer displays, typefaces with a constant thickness typically look better, so a sans-serif font such as Helvetica is likely a better choice than a serif font such as Times. Higher resolutions, together with antialiasing, increasingly make the difference a moot point, though; as always, the use made of the typeface (size, line spacing, etc.) is more important by far.

Should I include a footer on all slides, with title, speaker, slide number, etc.?

To constitute a worthwhile use of the slide's limited real estate, footers must prove useful during the presentation—and they seldom do. At best, a footer with title or speaker reassures the latecomers about being in the right room. Slide numbers may be useful for the audience to refer to a given slide when asking a question but often interfere visually with other content. A copyright notice appears best on handouts, which get distributed, not on projected slides.

Noise in presentation slides comes in many forms: unfamiliar fonts, unnecessary or aggressive colors, insufficient contrast between items and background, and, more generally, any feature used to decorate rather than convey meaning. More subtle, perhaps, is the case of slides having neither missing items nor superfluous ones, but simply looking wrong, largely because of suboptimal spatial arrangement.

Slides easily look disorganized when they display items that are visually uncoordinated (misaligned, meaninglessly different in size or aspect ratio, etc.).

Slides can look unbalanced when the space available is used poorly, for example when all the information appears on the far left, against a narrow left margin.

Slides can be confusing when they fail to structure the information visually, as with a tight list in which items do not stand out as distinct, despite bullets.

Constructing the slides

Although it never compensates for poor slide design, careful slide construction helps promote readability and maintain the attention of the audience by avoiding noise. Do more with less: use graphical features to convey meaning, not to try to wow your audience. Use a consistent slide layout throughout the presentation. Use one typeface and few sizes. Use colors sparingly: develop a first design in black and white, then add color in light touches, for emphasis or identification. Optimize each slide iteratively, challenging each feature in it.

Plan for a (very) wide left margin and set everything left against it.

Set your message at the top left, so it is prominent. Leave space for two lines of text (up to about 12 words) and generous margins.

If inexperienced in color design, use only one color besides black, possibly in a few different tints. Draw lines in a dark color or tint, and make them thick enough, too. Fill areas with a light color or tint; do not draw a frame around them.

Professionals write poorly, and that is understandable

They lack training
both in school and on the job

They lack examples
Poor writing reproduces by imitation

They lack motivation
They receive little feedback, if any

Optimize the line breaks by hand, to allow a faster, easier reading. Strive for meaningful line breaks as much as balanced line lengths.

Spread out the slide's main items, so that they stand out as distinct.

Reserve bullets for items in a list at levels below the topmost one. (Here, the items need no bullet.) Avoid bullets for isolated items and items not forming a true list.

Coordinate all sizes and positions, for structure and harmony.

Displayed lists
aligned left, with square bullets

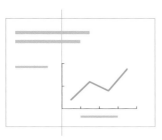

A single graph
aligned left, with label in margin

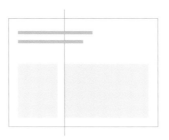

Two photographs
aligned far left, coordinated sizes

Displayed lists, with logo
all aligned left, including the title

*What if the screen is too large or too high
for me to point directly with my hand?*

If your slides stand on their own, you need not
point at the screen at all, really. In other words,
if your message depends on a given item being
highlighted at some point, build the highlight
in the slide itself, perhaps then as an animation.

If you nonetheless wish to point and the screen
is large, point with a stick, to control better
what the audience pays attention to. Pointing
with a laser beam or with a computer mouse
might put you out of the picture and turn you
into a "voice off": once they look at the screen,
the audience may well never look at you again,
for lack of a visible connection between the two.
When using a stick as pointer, plan for a place
to put it down whenever you do not need it,
so you can use your hands to make gestures
(and you do not fiddle with the pointer, either).

If the screen is too high for you to use a stick
and if you insist on pointing, consider a laser;
you are disconnected from the screen anyway.

Should I use computer animations?

Resist the temptation to include animations
just because you can with the tools you have;
use them when they help convey your message.
An animated graph that shows the evolution
of a curve over time may thus be enlightening;
in contrast, an item bouncing around the slide
is more likely to distract from the message.

Among the simple animations, slide build-ups
(making several items appear one at a time) can
help focus attention or reveal the complex. Still,
the fewer they are, the more impact they have.

Slides in a set must look consistent, not identical.
The corporate logo, for example, need not appear
on every slide—perhaps only on the first and last.
And structure slides—preview, transition, review—
can usefully stand out visually from content slides,
for example have a background of a different color
or all display the same picture. As a title, they can
repeat the presentation's title, possibly shortened,
instead of a less useful descriptor such as *preview*.

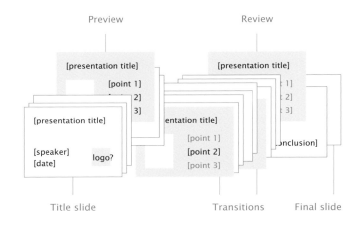

A title slide, including the speaker's name, the date,
etc., is helpful, even if the information it contains
must not be said orally (or at any rate not as such:
topic and speaker are clarified in the need and task).

The attention-getter slide, if any, should not be first,
lest it is seen before the speaker's very first words.
Place it after the title slide, and repeat the title slide
after it if you have no other slides until the preview.

A final slide after the conclusion slide can be useful
both to help close the presentation and to function
as low-noise "wallpaper" for questions and answers.
It could be no more than a (reasonable-size) logo,
centered, against an otherwise empty background.

Handling the slides

To AVOID COMPETING with the spoken text, slides must not only boast a visual design and low-noise construction but also be handled appropriately, both in space and in time.

In space, ensure both you and your slides are clearly visible. Before your presentation, adjust the equipment as required to get an image that is sharp, large enough, and high enough without being unnecessarily high. Whenever the setting allows, position yourself next to the projected slide; to draw attention to a given item on the slide, point at it directly with your hand. Look at your audience as much as possible, not at your slides, except briefly when pointing, so everyone follows your eyes. At all times, face your audience with shoulders, hips, and feet.

Look at your audience—not (or almost not) at your slides.

Point directly on the screen, using the hand on that side.

Face your audience squarely by placing your feet correctly.

In time, ensure your slides and spoken text are coordinated. Show each slide only when relevant. When changing slides, use a verbal transition. To be able to do so, be sure to know, at any point in your presentation, what the next slide is about: rehearse your presentation at least once without your slides.

While technology is usually best kept to a minimum (the less there is, the less likely it is that something goes wrong with it), a remote control to change slides is a worthwhile investment. It allows you to choose where to stand with fewer constraints and frees you from moving back and forth to change slides. Even so, remember to include transitions: these are not fillers; they are there to orient the audience to the material presented.

Delivering the presentation

ORAL PRESENTATIONS, in contrast to writing activities, are performances in real time. They indeed require that we master several components simultaneously: what we say (verbal delivery), how we say it (vocal delivery), and what we let our audience see about us (visual delivery). Each component can follow the three laws of communication.

Adapt to your audience while you deliver your presentation. Be receptive to the subtle nonverbal signals they send you, such as facial expressions or body postures: do they appear enlightened or confused, alert or tired, attentive or impatient? According to what you sense, you might explain differently, speed up or slow down, or perhaps even move closer to them.

Maximize the signal-to-noise ratio in each of the components. Above all, reduce the noise by avoiding distracting elements, even in codings not necessarily intended to convey a message, such as the way you dress: your audience should not notice your clothing, jewelry, or name tag instead of noticing you. Against the low-noise background, send loud and clear signals in all the components: clear, accurate, and concise wording, vocal variations that interpret and emphasize what you say, and a confident stance with visible and meaningful gestures.

Be effectively redundant across components. Convey meaning with well-chosen words, intonation, and appropriate gestures. Project confidence in what you say through a stable stance, a deep, steady vocal delivery, and sharp, deliberate gestures. Establish presence through a well-chosen position in the room, a tall, self-assured stance, and consistently strong eye contact.

While striving to master all components, do remain yourself. Through practice, automatize effective speaking behaviors so your mind is free to focus on your purpose and audience. Show interest in your topic and in the people in front of you. Establish a genuine relationship: speak *to* them, not *at* them.

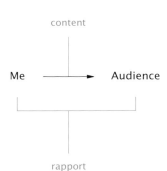

Delivering is more than supplying content blindly; it requires establishing rapport with an audience: a close and sincere relationship of mutual respect. Perhaps the simplest way to win the audience over is to show genuine interest in them and in the topic. When you care little about either audience or topic, you may end up giving an acceptable performance, but you cannot deliver an exceptional presentation. Great speakers are invariably passionate speakers.

Should I really never write out my text?

When every word matters, as when speaking on a sensitive topic and when being recorded, the advantages of a written text may outweigh its drawbacks. More than writing a text, though, endeavor to capture a "spoken text" on paper.

If you will be reading the text, practice doing so while maintaining frequent enough eye contact with the audience. Print the text large enough so you can read it easily without bending over, mark it up with vocal cues (such as emphasis), and slide the pages aside after reading them (do not turn them over, to avoid making noise).

Is it acceptable to have notes while I speak?

Having notes may reassure you but typically reduces your presence: holding notes hinders gestures; looking at notes breaks eye contact; reading notes interrupts the train of thought. For a short presentation or for one with slides, you should not need any (if you prepare well).

How should I handle a memory lapse?

A tree-like outline rather than a sequential one is your best strategy against memory lapses. Should you not remember one point, simply move on to the next one, without pointing this out to your audience. If you later remember the missing point, reinsert it as best you can, again without pointing the reorganization out.

If you are stuck in a sequence, recapitulating the points already covered will usually suffice to put your mind back on track, without giving your memory problem away to your audience.

Finding the right tone

As in written documents, a careful word selection makes for clear, accurate, concise presentations. What is just as important, it helps establish a tone that is appropriate to the occasion, thus speaking to your attitude toward both content and audience. If you are to get your message across effectively, beware of wording that weakens your statements, casts a doubt on your self-confidence, or otherwise undermines your image. Similarly, avoid wording that might antagonize or frustrate your audience when you can use more constructive alternatives. Below are examples of phrasing that will likely not convey the most favorable tone for your purpose.

I think that ... and other complex sentences that place their main information (which is often the message) in a subordinate clause.

I hope I have convinced you that ... and other clauses that express or suggest uncertainty about the effectiveness of the presentation.

This figure did not come out as I had hoped and other statements that point out flaws the audience might in fact not have noticed.

I will explain to you what the problems are and similar emphasis on *I* and *you* that might sound patronizing (better: *Let's see what* ...).

I just don't have time to explain how it works and other remarks announcing to listeners, to their frustration, what they will not be told.

If you nonetheless wish to let the audience know that you deliberately omit discussing a given point, offer them directions to it rather than a dead end. As usual, focus on your audience, not on yourself. Instead of *I don't have time to explain how it works*, you might say something like *You have all details about how it works in Appendix B of my handout.*

Optimizing verbal delivery

S POKEN TEXT DIFFERS from written text. For a natural style, speak ex tempore: know the outline of your presentation, but do not write out and memorize or read the exact wording, as it will probably sound like what it is: a recited written text. Instead, rehearse the presentation until you manage to express your points fluently in real time. When you speak ex tempore, you sound more genuine, you can adapt so much more easily to the situation, and you are less likely to forget what to say than when you memorize a text. To start and end confidently, you might memorize your very first and very last sentences.

The main verbal noise—and thus perhaps the delivery noise most easily noted by the audience—is the use of filler words: superfluous words such as *you know* or nonwords such as *um* that speakers utter when hesitating in their verbal delivery. Searching for one's words is normal when speaking ex tempore: fluency is not about always knowing what to say; it is about finding a suitable wording without any noticeable hesitation. A brief silence (a second or two) goes unnoticed and affords up to four times the thinking time of the average filler word. Even if it were noticed, it would likely be interpreted as a sign of careful word selection, entirely to the speaker's advantage. In fact, seasoned speakers sometimes make deliberate pauses while not having to look for words, as a rest for their audience. Silence is an ally, not an enemy; hence, eradicate filler words and learn to value those little silences in your presentations.

Rhetorical sentences (sentences that discuss the presentation as opposed to discussing the topic) are normally best avoided. Many of them, such as *I will mention advantages only briefly*, are simply unnecessary: be brief if you think you should be, but do not waste time announcing it, as it makes no difference for the audience to know it (if anything, it will frustrate them). Others, such as *I have drawn the evolution of it on this graph*, can usefully be replaced by sentences that convey a message, such as *As you can see, it first increases rapidly, but then* ....

I have a foreign accent. What can I do?

A slight accent is often regarded as charming, so do not worry excessively about it. Instead, just speak slowly, especially at the beginning, so your audience can get used to your accent. If you use slides, make sure that these include any key technical terms, to help your audience make the link with how you pronounce them.

I am told I speak too fast. What can I do?

Speaking fast is usually not a problem in itself; speaking fast *all the time* is the true problem: it puts both speaker and audience out of breath.

Rather than attempting to speak more slowly all the time, which is challenging, slow down deliberately and markedly at specific moments, for more complex or more important points: doing so brings useful contrast in your delivery and, of course, it reduces your mean vocal rate.

I am often not loud enough. What can I do?

Supervised breathing and speaking exercises may help you project your voice better. Still, if you fear the audience may not hear you well, arrange to have a microphone at your disposal.

To be fully visible and to be free to move about, prefer a mobile microphone to one that is fixed to a lectern; if possible, request a wireless one that you can clip onto your clothes, so you can use your hands to gesture or point at the screen. Try to keep your mouth at a constant distance from the microphone (or the other way around); specifically, beware of turning your head away from it, as when glancing at a projected slide.

Harnessing all three variables

Vocal delivery is a powerful yet often overlooked nonverbal coding, one that usefully complements visual delivery—or that must actually compensate for a lack of visual delivery whenever the speakers are no longer visible for any reason. To convince yourself of this power, think of how overwhelming it can be to hear again after a long time the voice of someone who used to be significant in your life.

Much of the usually limited advice on vocal delivery offered in school focuses on intonation. Teachers tell their students to avoid speaking in a monotone (an almost constant tone), which so easily prompts the listeners to nod off. In reaction, some students acquire an artificial tone, which makes them sound as if they are trying to recite a text learned by heart, instead of talking to their audience "here and now". The right intonation for a presentation is no different from that for a normal conversation—but amplified; that is, it need not be invented for the circumstance.

Because of a focus on intonation, many speakers overlook the next most important vocal variation: that of rate. Great intonation might be all it takes to keep the attention of the audience for a while but will simply not suffice for a longer presentation. Variation of rate—and pauses—will allow speaker and audience alike to go the distance without tiring, besides emphasizing complex or important parts.

Emphasis can be conveyed by variation of volume, too, and few speakers are aware of the wide range of acceptable volume: yes, you can go temporarily *much* louder or softer without being uncomfortable to listen to, and emphasize a point in proportion, at least as long as you do not overuse such a trick. To be effective, the variation must be deliberate, of course: many speakers tend to drop the volume accidentally on the last words of their sentences, sometimes to the point of making them inaudible, as they are already thinking of the next sentence.

Optimizing vocal delivery

V OCAL DELIVERY CAN BE CHARACTERIZED by tone, rate, and volume—all three under the control of the speaker to a large extent, in contrast to other qualities such as timbre. For an effective vocal delivery, apply the three laws to them. Adjust the mean value of your vocal tone, rate, and volume to the situation (first law). Around this constant mean value, introduce signal by modulating your tone, rate, and volume (second law). Do not vary your voice for its own sake, though; do it according to the meaning, complexity, and importance of what you say, as a form of effective redundancy (third law).

Tone

Tone conveys meaning, in a largely language-dependent way. Strive to speak around your natural mean tone; a higher tone, frequent under stress, would indeed betray your nervousness to your audience, particularly to those who know your voice. Around its mean, modulate your tone to reveal the meaning of what you say, such as going down at the end of a statement and up at the end of a question. In other words, just amplify the natural variations that come with the language you speak.

Rate

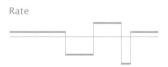

Beyond intonation, learn to control the rate at which you speak: it will open up a whole new dimension in your vocal delivery. On average, pace yourself (most people tend to speak faster when in front of an audience). Around this comfortable mean, modulate your rate according to complexity and importance: slow down for complex or important points and, conversely, feel free to speed up (reasonably) for what is at the same time less complex and less important. At any rate, do speak clearly.

Volume

Finally, you can convey emphasis with variations of volume, whether up or down. Speaking softer is actually a better way to quiet down noise from the audience than speaking louder. Sharp variations—all of a sudden, noticeably louder or softer— carry the strongest potential for regaining audience attention; overused, however, they lose impact and become bothersome. Speak loud whenever you think it appropriate, but never shout.

Should I really not move my legs at all?

Any unnecessary movement of the lower body, as when pacing, fidgeting, or shifting weight from one leg to the other, immediately reveals a speaker's uneasiness, undermining credibility. Hence, do not move hips, legs, or feet at all—unless doing so carries meaning. For example, you might move on your transitions to explain each point from a different place in the room (a meaningful but not straightforward move) or even make a gesture with your whole body.

Is it acceptable to put my hands in my pockets?

Having one's hands in one's pockets might be thought of as nonchalant, yet the impression of nonchalance results from the overall stance, such as one with the shoulders clearly sagging, and not from the hands alone. Having one hand in a pocket while the other points at the screen is usually not frowned upon as inappropriate if the speaker stands with shoulders straight.

Still, beware of what your hands might fiddle with in your pockets, such as coins and keys. Emptying your pockets before a presentation is thus a good habit: it reduces the risk of noise.

How can I look at everyone in a large audience?

If the audience is large, look at every part of it, as opposed to everyone in it. To this purpose, you might divide the room mentally in blocks: back left, back center, back right, front left, etc. Within each block, do look at specific persons in the eyes whenever possible. Remember also to move your whole head, not just your eyes, as you make eye contact with different blocks.

Setting the stage

Rational speakers often concentrate their attention on the verbal component. Yet nonverbal codings, and visual delivery in particular, carry much power in terms of establishing—or destroying—credibility.

A first step toward effective visual communication, one too often overlooked by speakers, is to set up the room. Many rooms are suboptimal by default and can usefully be rearranged or at least tidied up, to be rid of visual distractions. Not all rooms are available ahead of time for optimization, of course, but you can always ask what is possible. Ideally, you would select yourself the most suitable room for your purpose, particularly one of the right size. Physical proximity both among audience members and with the speaker makes for a warm atmosphere.

The second step is to choose where you will stand. If you are to impress the audience with your body (in a sense, that is), you must be visible. To avoid becoming a mere "voice off" when projecting slides, you must be close to the screen; lights must be on. If you are not using slides, you may want to stand closer to your audience, physically and figuratively. If you hide behind an otherwise reassuring lectern (usually far away from both screen and audience), you thus fail to capitalize on your physical presence.

The third step, then, is to maintain your visibility where you are. Make your gestures not only large but also high enough, so everyone can see them. Also, bring your hands down when not gesturing, so your gestures stand out even more in contrast. Look at your audience, so that they look at you, too.

If you are delivering together with another speaker, make eye contact with the audience when you have the floor only. When not speaking, look at the one who is speaking: audience members looking at you will follow your eyes and look at the other speaker. (Alternatively, go sit in the room to be out of sight.)

Optimizing visual delivery

A WELL-CONTROLLED VISUAL DELIVERY projects confidence; it thus goes a long way toward convincing the audience of what is being said. This projected confidence results largely from presence (a question of signal), stability (a lack of noise), and sincerity, as perceived in the match (effective redundancy) between the verbal and nonverbal components of the delivery. It requires constant control of one's body—from toe to head.

Look at your audience (everyone, at all times, straight in the eyes).

Make large, deliberate gestures (and no noise between gestures).

Stand tall, straight, and... stable (particularly in your lower body).

For a confident stance, first decide where you will be standing, go there, and... stay there. Plant your feet firmly on the floor, a little bit apart for stability and easier abdominal breathing, and distribute your weight equally on both legs. Hold the pose: do not dissipate nervous energy into meaningless movements, mostly of the lower body. Stand tall and straight, yet not stiff. Strive to look rock solid; so will the material you present, too.

In contrast, feel free to use your hands—in a meaningful way, needless to say: make large, deliberate gestures as you see fit to illustrate or emphasize what you say. When not gesturing, make no noise: return your hands to a stable, neutral position, for example alongside your body or perhaps behind your back. Avoid any form of mannerism giving your nervousness away, such as rubbing your hands. Avoid temptations, too: remove what you might fiddle with, such as a pen, a ring, or a bracelet.

Besides with your hands, send strong signals with your face. Facial expressions convey emotions—better than words, too. Are you perhaps concerned, surprised, or enthused? Do you want to tell it to the audience? Let them know with your face (and, if appropriate, also with words, for effective redundancy).

Finally, and besides your suitable position and stable stance, command attention by making eye contact with the audience: look at everyone (as far as possible); look at all times (as often as possible, that is); look at them straight in the eyes. If you do, they simply cannot ignore you. Eye contact is powerful stuff.

Eliminating noisy habits

I am an experienced speaker. Need I rehearse?

Rehearsing is the best way, if not the only way, to estimate how long a presentation will take. Moreover, even experienced speakers seldom come up with the best phrasing the first time. Exceptional speakers typically rehearse more, not less, than average ones. Every detail counts.

How many times should I rehearse?

You should rehearse as many times as needed to reach the level of quality that you have set for yourself and for that specific presentation. In some cases, it might take just a few times; in other cases, or for the more difficult parts of the presentation, it might take many times.

Is there no risk of rehearsing too much?

If you feel that you are losing your spontaneity, you might not have rehearsed enough, really. Indeed, genuine is not the same as ingenuous: you can prepare every aspect of a presentation and still remain yourself, by showing genuine interest in both your topic and your audience.

Should I rehearse with a test audience?

A test audience can usefully ask test questions and provide feedback, but its artificiality may affect your rehearsal. Do what works for you. A test audience need not be large to be helpful.

To practice eye contact without a real audience, just have several pairs of eyes looking at you. Teddy bears make a patient practice audience. So do portraits of people looking at the camera.

Through practice, you will surely improve in time, although you may not make any conscious effort other than endeavoring to do your best. To a point, you improve without being aware of how you do it: intuitively, you just get the knack of it after a while.

Not everything, alas, comes intuitively to speakers. Some behaviors (if not all of them, beyond a point) require a conscious effort to be further improved. The effort thus required is usually intense enough that little attention can be devoted to other aspects. Hence, the undesired behavior must be eliminated once and for all, and the desired one automatized, so speakers can concentrate on the occasion again.

To eliminate an undesired, unconscious behavior, introduce a feedback loop to become aware of it and focus on improving it during dedicated practice.

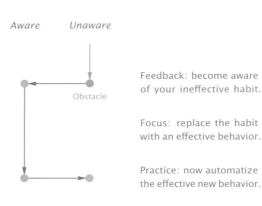

Feedback: become aware of your ineffective habit.

Focus: replace the habit with an effective behavior.

Practice: now automatize the effective new behavior.

As an example, suppose that you want to eliminate a filler word, such as *um*. Do the following exercise: gather a mini-audience and ask them to propose simple topics on which you are to speak impromptu, striving not to say *um*; ask them to let you know whenever you do, for example by raising a finger. Keep going: do not worry about other problems, do not feel guilty or apologize when you say *um*. Soon enough, the filler word should be controlled.

Getting ready for the presentation

GREAT SPEAKERS ARE BORN, NOT MADE—or so they say. Exceptional delivery requires an exceptional personality, this much is true, for oral communication reveals who one is. Still, being an exceptional speaker is not a purpose in itself: most everyone can learn to deliver well enough to be effective.

You can always improve your delivery by practicing regularly and by rehearsing each presentation as many times as needed. Regular practice will sharpen your speaking skills in general, so look for opportunities, big or small, to speak for an audience (do not wait until you are faced with a critical presentation). Rehearsals allow you, by trial and error, to express your ideas more clearly, more accurately, and, especially, more concisely, to come up with appropriate vocal modulation and gestures, and to adjust the amount of material to the target duration. Moreover, they boost your confidence about the presentation by eliminating unknowns, thus helping improve your delivery.

Beyond the initial, often piecemeal, phase of trial and error, rehearse your presentation in as realistic a way as possible. Choose an appropriate setting: use the room you will speak in, when available; create (or imagine) a plausible one otherwise. Rehearse at least once as if you were in front of the audience: out loud, standing up, using verbal, vocal, and visual delivery, handling your slides, pointing on a (real or imaginary) screen. Pay special attention to transitions, rate variations, gestures: if they do not come easily to you in real time, plan each one ahead of time; then rehearse them until they fit in smoothly.

On the day of the presentation, come early and come prepared. Allow plenty of time to set up the room and the equipment, and foresee an alternative for anything that might go wrong, most notably technology. Adjust your appearance, if needed, before the audience walks in: once they see you, you are on. An oral presentation is physically and nervously demanding, so come rested. If you have to speak after a meal, eat lightly.

How long your presentation lasts when you are rehearsing it alone is but an indication of how long it will last in front of an audience. Most people tend to speak faster or forget details under pressure; others, however, are stimulated by an audience and speak longer.

With experience, you can figure your personal "correction factor" to anticipate the actual duration from that of your final rehearsal.

Taking no chances

How should I handle a mistake?

If you make a mistake, do correct it. As a rule, however, refrain from apologizing. By drawing attention to a shortcoming that the audience might otherwise not have noted (if corrected), apologies distract much more than they help. Though well-meant, they are a source of noise.

How long in advance should I be in the room?

Being in the room early has a double purpose: making sure that everything is as it should be and becoming familiar with the room. Hence, how long in advance you should be in the room is dictated by how much time you anticipate needing to reach these purposes. If you must rearrange tables and chairs or test equipment, being there an hour early is not unreasonable: it leaves time for trials and errors, if required. Ideally, both room and speaker must be ready before any member of the audience walks in.

How about taking alcohol to calm my nerves?

Alcohol (or other tranquilizers) might indeed ease your anxiety and thus feel a welcome aid. Alas, they typically reduce your alertness, too, or even make you lose touch with the audience. If you want to be in control, and you typically do for an oral presentation, stay away from alcohol.

Anxiety gives me a dry mouth. What can I do?

To reactivate the natural production of saliva, try biting your tongue (gently) or pressing it against your teeth. (Drinking water, in contrast, will bring temporary symptomatic relief only.)

Addressing an audience is a daunting experience for most people, yet many of these disregard some of the most basic steps toward ensuring success and, by the same token, moderating their anxiety. While an oral presentation is a real-time exercise, its success is largely determined by all that is done ahead of time, down to the last detail. Be prepared.

To boost your confidence, speak on familiar ground. Always come early and make the room your room: do not just take it as it comes, no questions asked. Rearrange tables and chairs as you would like them. Try out the markers for the whiteboard or flip chart. Test all technology (projector, microphone, lights, temperature control, etc.) and adjust it as you see fit. Have someone assist you if needed, but get it done. Deciding that taking care of rooms is not your job will do you no good when something goes wrong.

One way of eliminating unknowns and, to a point, technological risks is to use your own equipment. Although it may not be practical to carry or install your own video projector each time, you might insist on connecting your own computer or remote control. More simply, you might come with a bottle of water at room temperature, to take a sip before you start, instead of drinking their ice-cold water. You might also replace the markers in the room with your own, not only because you know yours are a fresh set, but also because yours feel familiar in your hand.

The comfort that comes from feeling one's own whiteboard markers in one's hand is almost ritual. Other such habits can help, especially if associated with positive memories. You might want to wear your lucky shirt for the occasion. As you get ready, you might listen to your favorite song or indulge in a piece of candy. (In contrast, this is probably not the day to wear your new shoes for the first time, be on a tight schedule, or drink too much coffee.) Such rituals help you feel on familiar ground, too.

Managing stage fright

ANXIETY BEFORE and perhaps during an oral presentation is a reassuring phenomenon: it indicates that you care, and you should if you are to deliver an effective presentation. By releasing adrenaline in your blood, it makes you more alert and prepares your organism for the upcoming energy demand. Stage fright should therefore not be suppressed but managed. Welcome it as a positive symptom—and feel no guilt about it.

Much anxiety comes from a fear of the unknown. To manage your stage fright ahead of time, eliminate as many unknowns as possible. Prepare and rehearse the presentation carefully. Meet the audience in advance. Take possession of the room: make it yours by setting it up to your liking and by being in it early enough to become familiar with it and test the equipment.

To relieve somewhat the restlessness induced by adrenaline, pace your breathing. Just before delivering the presentation, take two slow, deep breaths. If you seem to get out of breath at any time, make a pause and, again, take a slow, deep breath. Striving to speak slowly and softly might calm you down, too.

As one step toward being positive (and unless inappropriate, given the content of your presentation), smile at your audience. A smile helps make everyone feel good, starting with yourself. It works across cultures, it can be noticed all the way from the back row, and it even improves your voice.

Overall, have a positive image of yourself and of the situation. See the presentation as an opportunity rather than an ordeal, and focus on your purpose and your audience, not on yourself. Should something not go as planned, waste no energy blaming yourself; instead, look for another way of achieving the same. See yourself succeeding. If all you can visualize is yourself failing miserably, part of you may well try to prove you right. Think of what you need to do, not of what you want to avoid.

Respect your audience and your audience will respect you, too; after all, they have very little to gain from a poor presentation, so they want you to succeed. As an essential form of respect, always be yourself: do not pretend to be someone you are not. Show your best self (do not put yourself down), but be genuine. As long as you visibly do your best, not much can go wrong.

Answering questions

QUESTIONS ARE TYPICALLY the part of the presentation that speakers hate or fear the most. Not being known ahead of time, they can induce considerable stress, because they require that speakers think on their feet. Yet they do not entirely escape the control of speakers either, for speakers can prepare themselves to handle questions well. Moreover, questions are an opportunity more than a threat: they often represent a second chance to get messages across. Second chances are all too rare, so they should be welcomed.

You can prepare for questions at two levels: content and form. To prepare for what to answer (content), anticipate questions first of all by putting yourself in the shoes of your audience: what might they want to know that you did not already include in your presentation? You can also practice for a test audience representative of, or able to role-play, your actual audience, and invite them to ask you questions (do keep track of these). To prepare for how to answer (form), rehearse your answers to the questions you anticipate. If appropriate, create slides. Sharpen your impromptu speaking skills through practice, too.

1	**Listen** to the whole question, to ensure you understand it.
2	**Repeat / rephrase** as needed, so others understand it, too.
3	**Think** to construct an answer that is brief and to the point.
4	**Answer** to the whole audience, keeping eye contact with all.

When taking a question, do not rush to answer. First, increase the chance you understand the exact question by listening to it: resist the urge to interrupt the questioner as soon as you think you know what the question is. Second, ensure the audience is with you, too: if not everyone heard it, repeat the question; if you fear not everyone understood it, rephrase the question. Third, and even when you believe you know the answer, think: take time to construct an answer that is brief and to the point. Finally, deliver this answer to your whole audience: endeavor to make eye contact with everyone, not just with the questioner.

Unless the session is chaired by someone else, stay in charge. Indicate clearly who is invited to ask his or her question next. If you receive several questions at once from the same person, clarify which question you are answering by repeating it first.

What if I do not get any questions?

Do not assume too readily that the audience has no questions, just because no one seems to want to ask one: most people simply dislike going first. Give them time. Encourage them nonverbally by looking and by smiling at them. Invite them verbally, too, perhaps with a touch of humor if it is your style (*Ah, come on, now: who is bold enough to ask the first question?*). If there are still no questions, close the session.

What if I do not understand the question?

If you did not hear the question, move closer to the person and ask him or her to repeat it, speaking louder. If you did not understand it, ask the person to rephrase it. (If unsuccessful after several attempts, for example because of a foreign accent, ask the audience for help.) If you think you understood the question but are not sure, rephrase it for the whole audience, then ask the questioner, *Is this your question?*

What if the question is not a question?

If someone makes a comment, do not answer: simply thank him or her for the contribution, then invite the audience again to ask questions.

Should the comment become annoyingly long for the audience, as when it is beside the point, try to regain control of the session. Usually, then, you must interrupt—a delicate operation. Attempt it nonverbally first: break eye contact or show your intent with a gesture of the hand. If unsuccessful, try it verbally, first tentatively, then more deliberately. By proceeding tactfully, you will gain the esteem of the whole audience.

The impact of even the most effective presentation can suffer severely from poorly handled questions, leaving the audience with a bad overall impression. Just because you can seldom rehearse your answers does not mean delivery no longer matters for them. Keep concentrating all the way to the last question to maintain the delivery level of your presentation. Having to think on your feet is all the more reason to strive to automatize effective delivery behaviors (verbal, vocal, visual) through dedicated exercises.

To answer briefly and to the point, take your time; rushing in is by no means a hallmark of expertise. Make sure you understand the question precisely; if needed, ask for clarification (*Do you mean ...?*). Give yourself the time to find an effective wording and, more important still, to structure your answer and to make this structure clear to your audience, for example by announcing the various parts of it (*There are two reasons, really, why we ... First, ...*). For simple questions, consider the PREP structure.

Point	State your position in a few words (perhaps as briefly as *yes* or *no*).
Rationale	Support your point conceptually with one or more reasons for it.
Example	Illustrate your point in practice, to make it clear and memorable.
Point	State your position one last time, to bring about a sense of closure.

Keep your answers brief, especially if the audience is large or the question-and-answer period is short. Not everyone is interested in every question asked and some may be waiting to ask their own question. If you can, remain available after the presentation for those who did not have the opportunity to ask their question or perhaps prefer to ask it in private.

This question is somewhat off topic and requires a long answer. Perhaps the two of us can discuss it after the presentation or during the coffee break?

Difficult questions, such as a question that is off topic or one that you do not know the answer to, may take you by surprise but are not terribly hard to handle, except for the hostile ones. As a rule, be honest and helpful. Dare to say things the way they are, but always strive to help, not offend, the questioner.

A question that is off topic or that has been covered already in the presentation (perhaps before the questioner came in) is not likely to interest the audience at large. Feel free to flag the question as such—respectfully—or answer it very briefly, perhaps referring to your presentation when restating points, then offer to provide a longer answer privately at a later time.

I do not have those data with me, but if you give me your card, I will be happy to e-mail you the answer.

This question falls outside my own area of research, but perhaps someone in the room has an answer?

I would not know for sure, as I have never actually computed it, but if I had to guess, I would say ...

A question that you do not know the answer to is unpleasant: it often revives the guilt engraved by a school system in which not knowing the answer was bad. Contrary to school masters, however, real-world audiences ask questions, not to test you on something they know, but to learn something they do not. Instead of feeling guilty, focus on helping them out. Do admit, as constructively as you can, that you do not know the answer; then strive to find one: ask if anyone in the audience knows, propose to research the answer and provide it later, or perhaps offer your best guess (make it clear, then, that it is only a guess).

I understand your concern about our using animals in our laboratories. As you know, however, we are testing a therapy for cancer, so we must balance this animal suffering with human suffering. [ideal]

I can see that you feel strongly about unnecessary animal suffering. I am therefore happy to report that all our animal experiments take place under strict supervision by an ethical committee. [fact]

I hear what you say. It is, however, not a question but rather your personal opinion—and I respect it. Yet we at [company name] think differently about it.

A hostile question will likely hurt, no matter how proficient a speaker you become: to be proficient, you must be sensitive. Remain calm: if you attack one person, for whatever reason, you may well lose the whole audience. Quiet the atmosphere by marking a pause before answering: silence works wonders. Then address the question calmly at a double level: emotional and intellectual. First, acknowledge the concern. In most cases, people shout to be heard; they attack others when feeling hurt. Let the person know you have heard him or her; show empathy. Next, feel free to disagree with the opinion, referring to ideals or to well-established facts. If it is a simple matter of opinion, just say your opinion (or that of your organization) is different.

"What is the use of a book," thought Alice,
"without pictures or conversations?"

— Lewis Carroll

I have found that all ugly things are made
by those who strive to make something beautiful,
and that all beautiful things are made
by those who strive to make something useful.

— Oscar Wilde

Effective graphical displays

GRAPHICAL DISPLAYS complement verbal discourse in written documents and in oral presentations as a most powerful form of effective redundancy. Through spatial relationships and potential richness of detail, they provide insights in ways that text cannot hope to match. They include not only illustrations such as drawings, graphs, and photographs, but also the visual appearance of anything that can be seen, such as a printed page or a presentation slide.

Because they are in essence nonsequential, visual components are more difficult to analyze and to design than verbal ones. No methodology can state what type of information to locate in the beginning, middle, and end of a true graphical display, for visual codings simply have no beginning, middle, or end. This part first proposes alternative descriptions of pictures. Focusing on the display of numbers, it then discusses how to plan, design, and construct graphs, and how to add captions.

Understanding pictures

This photograph of a late-night cup of herbal tea (together with someone smiling in anticipation) includes many distracting items: two objects on the counter, a bag on the floor, and an overall slope.

This revised version is less noisy. The cup would look better still with its handle visible on the side and the tea-bag label closer to it.

PICTURES (VISUAL REPRESENTATIONS) take many forms: they can thus be drawings, graphs, or photographs, or just the visual appearance of pages in a document. All these pictures share the characteristics of visual codings, being intuitive and global in contrast to rational and sequential. Accordingly, they can be processed considerably faster than, and to some extent concurrently with, verbal codings (text). They are also essentially concrete and, to a point, ambiguous.

As usual, the way a representation is processed by the brain matters more than the way it is perceived by the senses. Thus, this processing is a better basis than production technology (drawing, photograph, etc.) for devising a typology of pictures that helps us choose "the right picture" for a given purpose. The choice between a drawing and a photograph, for example, is not nearly as decisive as their respective degrees of realism.

Beyond selecting the best visual representation for a purpose, one can optimize the representation selected, among others, to ensure that it is truly visual—in other words, that it matches human intuition. Web icons and road signs, for example, even those including no word, are not as visual as they appear when they rely on conventions of shape, color, or orientation. A convention may well be needed, but it is often not intuitive, to the extent that it must be learned: it is rational knowledge.

Just like text, and as a second-draft optimization, a picture can be made concise by the removal of unnecessary items: distracting objects, persons, or background in a photograph, unneeded lines, shapes, or colors in a graph or a diagram, etc. A picture is complete once nothing can be suppressed in it.

The above discussion applies to all pictures, including those representing quantitative information: graphs, too, must use the right representation for their purpose, audience, and data, and must be optimized to be intuitive and visually concise.

Conveying concepts visually

*On the scale of pictorialness,
what are abstract pictures?*

An abstract visual representation would be one
that does not resemble (or no longer resembles)
what it represents, as far as the audience can tell.
One example is the symbol for the planet Mars,
♂, originally depicting Mars's shield and spear.
Except for those who might readily recognize
its representational origin, this symbol is now
an abstract picture, with conventional meaning.

*If conventional codings (or abstract pictures)
are like words, are they useful at all?*

Conventional pictures, like words, do require
an entry in some sort of a mental dictionary.
They are nevertheless nonverbal in the sense
that they are not part of a language. A red circle
with red diagonal can thus be used in common
across languages more easily than words can.
Also, it is processed globally, not sequentially
like a word within a sentence, thus it can still
combine intuitively with other visual elements.
For the same reason, it does not combine well
with words into a sequential pseudosentence.
The sign on the left (below) may be misleading:
approaching motorists might see and identify
the *no right turn* visual coding before they are
even close enough to be able to read the text.
Redundant codings, as on the sign on the right,
work better: each makes full sense on its own.

ON RED

pseudosentence

NO RIGHT
TURN

redundant codings

Conveying a concept with a visual representation
is often desirable, for example to clarify meaning
across languages or illustrate messages on slides,
yet it is difficult, because pictures are intrinsically
concrete and ambiguous. A verbal statement (text)
next to the picture, ensuring effective redundancy,
is all the more needed when the concept is generic.

The context often clarifies the intended meaning,
but it may not suffice, and relying on it may be risky.
A slide showing a mobile phone crossed out in red,
on the screen when the audience enters the room,
will likely be interpreted as *switch off your phone*
(the intended meaning), not as *no phones allowed*.
A drawing more effectively encompasses all makes
and models, but even a photograph would likely
prompt everyone to switch off their mobile phones
(not just the owners of the specific model shown).
In contrast, a photograph of a shiny green apple
shown in a red circle with red diagonal is ambiguous
even within the context of an airport's arrival hall.
What specifically is prohibited entry into the country?
Shiny green apples? Apples? Fruit? Fresh produce?
Lifting the ambiguity is not straightforward, though,
even with a line drawing instead of a photograph.
Suppose the intended meaning here is *no fresh fruit*:
how to draw fruit generically without representing
a specific type of fruit such as an apple or a banana?
One approach is to show different fruits together,
but it makes the representation visually complex.

Conventional representations such as crossing out
help convey abstract meaning such as *no* or *don't*,
but assume common knowledge from the viewers,
which is not obvious with international audiences
and partly defeats the purpose of using a picture.
As an example, a U-shaped arrow in a red circle is
interpreted as *U-turn forbidden* in the Netherlands
but *U-turn allowed* in Chile, where the convention
for *forbidden* is found in the red diagonal only, used
redundantly with the red circle in many countries.

Choosing the right picture

Pictures can be classified along two scales: a picture is more or less *pictorial* (resembling what it represents) and more or less *literal* (intended to mean what it represents). Although these two scales are in essence continuous, each can usefully be divided into three categories, for ease of selection.

Pictures can be realistic, schematic, or abstract (*pictorialness*). Schematic pictures work remarkably well. Line drawings thus typically represent abstract concepts better than photographs: by abstracting much of the irrelevant visual detail unavoidably present in a photograph, they are usually far less distracting. By contrast, photographs more easily convey an atmosphere, thanks to their visual richness and their high level of realism.

Pictures have literal, metaphorical, or conventional meaning (*literalness*). At the literal (or iconic) level, a picture of an apple just means an apple. At the metaphorical (or indexical) level, it means something akin to an apple: tempting like an apple, such as sin, culturally related to an apple, such as education in the United States, etc. At the conventional (or symbolic) level, it may mean a record label or a consumer electronics company. While remaining a tangible coding (it still looks like an apple), the symbolic apple is much closer to a word than to a picture.

The fact that pictures can be interpreted more or less literally can cause confusion. First, the less literal the representation, the more likely the misunderstanding, unless the convention is well-known to the audience or is made explicit, as by a text. Still, graphical conventions are usually proper to subcultures, not to languages, so audience familiarity with them is difficult to gauge. Second, even when viewers can interpret a picture correctly at various levels of literalness, they might not know which level is intended. For example, does a picture of a key literally mean a key or metaphorically mean the act of locking, or a metal object, or a solution? The context helps determine the intended level but usually cannot lift the ambiguity fully.

	Realistic	Schematic
Conventional (symbolic)	Apple Records	Apple Inc.
Metaphorical (indexical)	Sin	Education
Literal (iconic)	Specific apple	Generic apple

Labeling illustrations

Is an illustration still "truly visual" if it includes words, such as labels?

Admittedly, words have an arbitrary meaning that must be (or has been) learned rationally; they are not intuitive like a photograph can be. Words used as labels on an illustration, however, are seen in isolation, not as part of a sentence, so they are processed largely nonsequentially: labels can be read in any order and at any time, because each label conveys meaning on its own. If the words used are familiar to the audience, they therefore hardly harm the global character of the illustration, and in any case much less than a legend, which requires that the audience learn a new "dictionary" prior to interpreting the illustration—a demanding mental process.

In a scatter plot showing subsets, how can I avoid using a legend?

To interpret a scatter plot displaying subsets, as with different data markers, the audience must indeed learn what marker is what subset. Still, rather than including a separate legend, try labeling one data marker for each subset on the graph itself: such labels are admittedly nothing but a distributed legend, but they are at hand when the audience needs them most, namely when looking at the data in the graph.

In a line plot, how can I label lines that almost overlap?

If data lines almost overlap, they will be hard to tell apart, no matter what you do. Question the need to tell them apart, given the message. If you feel you must label them, try connecting each label to its data line with a (discreet) line.

Effective graphical displays are visual, not verbal: they do not rely on symbolic meaning and can thus be interpreted correctly without a sequential step. As a counterexample, legends, being conventional, turn graphs into something to read, not something to look at: after viewing a pie chart with a legend, people remember a segment as being "the red one" or "the one on the left" (something they have seen), but they often cannot associate it with its meaning in the legend (something they should have read), all the more so if they were listening to a speaker while viewing the chart on screen. Direct labeling works better: the association between pie segment and matching meaning is immediate and intuitive, being based on proximity, not arbitrary color code.

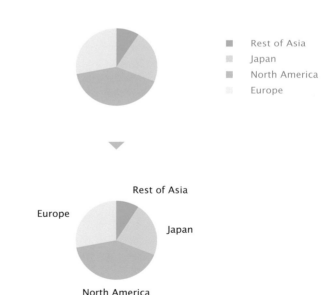

As a rule, avoid legends. Label all your illustrations (schematic diagrams, line plots, scatter plots, etc.) by placing the necessary words where they belong: next to the items they describe or visibly connected to these items, as with a thin line. In other words, keep illustrations visual, that is, global and intuitive.

Matching human intuition

What do you see primarily:
five rows or five columns?

Most probably columns,
because of proximity

Most probably rows,
because of similarity

Truly visual representations are in essence intuitive: they require no new interpretation rules, no verbal steps. Instead, they are based, among others, on four intuitive rules, interpreting *proximity*, *similarity*, *prominence*, and *sequence*. These rules are not independent of one another: prominence can thus result from distance, difference, or lack of sequence.

Proximity suggests connection, two items closer to each other being more tightly connected. Proximity is the basis of layout: it structures information by clustering items at various levels, makes items stand out by setting them off from all the others, identifies items in a graphical display with adjacent labels, etc. Combined with other structuring features, such as alignment, it can suggest one or more processing sequences on the page.

Similarity of visual appearance suggests similarity of meaning or function. Accordingly, identical items are best displayed identically, similar items similarly, different items differently. The more visual features are involved to mark the difference (shape, color, size, etc.), the more prominent the difference is.

Prominence suggests relative importance, a matter of contrast. Words set larger typically indicate a higher level of heading in a written document and the key statement (the message) on a slide used in an oral presentation. In graphical displays, a thicker line similarly suggests more important items or data, hierarchically or contentwise. Besides size, prominence may stem from color, shape, position, demarcation, distance, etc.

Sequence in space suggests continuity, structure, or possibly sequence in time. A spatial organization, as with alignments, suggests a similar organization in contents—a visual structure. Accidental near-alignment too often looks like misalignment. In the absence of another visual sequence, a detailed display will likely be scanned in the same pattern as text (for example, first left to right, then top to bottom for the English language).

Are length representations best displayed horizontally (bars) or vertically (columns)?

Horizontal segments (bars) are usually easier to label or to combine with a table, so they are a useful default. Vertical segments (columns) more easily suggest an evolution in function of a continuous variable. Such an evolution is however better served by markers positioned along a scale and perhaps connected by a line.

Must bars (columns) always start from zero?

Bars are interpreted as a length representation: their lengths must be proportional to the data they encode, lest they misrepresent these data. In other words, they must necessarily extend from zero on the corresponding scale indeed. Bars not starting from zero are a graphical lie.

Of course, the zero value must be meaningful, not arbitrary as with degrees of temperature, and the length representation must be linear: bars along a logarithmic scale are meaningless.

How about interrupting overly long bars?

Overly long bars may indeed needlessly reduce the resolution for the other bars in the display. Interrupting these bars visually is one solution. Another is having two graphs at different scales, which may give a fuller, more correct picture: one graph showing all bars, another excluding the outliers to zoom in on the rest of the data.

If you interrupt a bar, make this interruption conspicuous, and interrupt the scale as well. If there is no scale, indicate the numerical value of the interrupted bar next to the end of the bar.

Bars—too often a default choice—are inappropriate when they run along a nonlinear scale or do not start from a meaningful zero position. For many data sets, they are best replaced by a position representation.

A position representation need not start from zero, but one starting close to zero can mislead viewers, especially if the axes intersect. The range is then best extended to zero, for a more intuitive display.

A concurrent variation in two (or more) directions results in a hard-to-compare area representation.

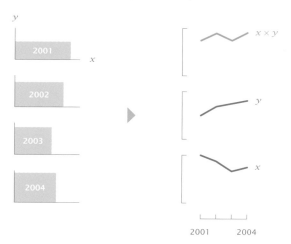

Representing quantitative data

QUANTITATIVE DISPLAYS (graphs) are metaphorical maps, in which some geometrical magnitudes are proportional to the respective data they are meant to represent graphically. Yet not all magnitudes are equally intuitive or equally accurate. Variations in one dimension, coded as a length or a position, are more accurately perceived than those involving estimates in two or more dimensions, as for angles, areas, and volumes.

A length representation, in the form of lines, bars, or columns, offers a straightforward comparison of data in a (limited) set: it is intuitive and accurate, especially with the lengths aligned at one end. For these lengths to be proportional to the data, the scale must run from zero, thereby bounding the resolution.

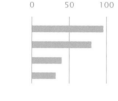

Slightly less intuitive, a position representation along a scale offers the highest resolution of the data set (at fixed graph size, that is), because the range used need no longer start from zero. Intuition and accuracy must be balanced for an optimal graph: ranges that extend almost to zero may as well start from zero. Similarly, because axes that cross strongly suggest an origin (zero-zero position), axes not including zero should not cross.

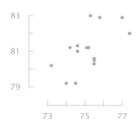

An angle or slope representation is less accurately perceived than a linear representation (length or position along a scale). Though intuitive, a pie chart thus fails to resolve close values. Likewise, a slope (a ratio of two variations) is more accurately viewed as a direct linear representation of the first derivative.

An area representation is even less accurate. It is best avoided, unless as an implicit integral (area under a curve); in this case, the range must include zero, as in any length representation. When accuracy matters, an integral is best displayed explicitly, for example as a position representation, just like a derivative.

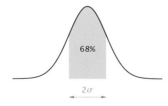

Volumes drawn in perspective are by far the most inaccurate of quantitative displays and are best replaced by alternatives.

Planning the graph

GRAPHS, MORE THAN documents or presentations, may be generated for oneself rather than for an audience, that is, for analysis rather than for communication. All the same, they do require careful planning to be effective. Together with the intended message or the research question, the structure of the data set (number and nature of variables) is what most largely dictates the type of graph to be selected.

Graphs, just like paragraphs, are meant to convey messages or, equivalently, to answer questions about the data displayed. Questions usually involve comparison among individual data, distribution of data along a scale, correlation among variables, or evolution (over time) of a variable. Almost at a metalevel, they might also involve comparison among subsets of data, that is, a comparison of different comparisons, distributions, correlations, or evolutions, often requiring complex displays.

Patient	Gender	Weight [kg]	Conc. [ng/ml]
1	female	75	31.3
2	male	81	16.5
3	female	52	11.8
4	female	69	39.5
5	male	65	8.0
6	female	83	22.7
7	male	64	14.0
⋮	⋮	⋮	⋮

Discrete variable   Continuous variables

Variables can be continuous or discrete. Continuous variables represent series of numbers that can assume, at least in theory, all possible values, such as measurements of the temperature. They run along either an interval scale, with an arbitrary zero, such as degree Celsius, or a ratio scale, with an absolute zero, such as Kelvin. Discrete variables represent series of labels, dividing the data into subsets. They are located along either a nominal scale, such as gender (the values *male* and *female* cannot be ordered), or an ordinal scale, such as drug dosage (*control*, *low*, *medium*, and *high* can meaningfully be ordered).

Like any structure, that of the data set is a view of the mind. As an example, with properties measured at both 30 and 80°C, temperature can be regarded as either a continuous variable (with, as it happens, two actual values only) or a discrete one (with "30°C" and "80°C" seen as labels, not numerical values). Similarly, the conductivity of materials *a*, *b*, and *c* can be seen as three distinct continuous variables or as one (conductivity) plus one discrete variable (material type, with labels *a*, *b*, *c*).

Designing the graph

T HE OPTIMAL GRAPH DESIGN depends on two factors, primarily: the message to be conveyed to the audience or, equivalently, the research question to be answered and the structure of the data set (the variables to be shown). The number of continuous variables dictates the basic designs that most effectively answer each of the four types of question.

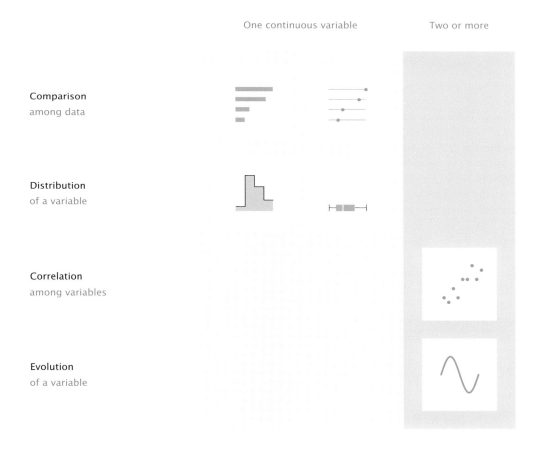

One continuous variable   Two or more

Comparison
among data

Distribution
of a variable

Correlation
among variables

Evolution
of a variable

Once a design is selected, discrete variables can be rendered as subsets within one panel or as a display of several panels of the same design (or perhaps as a combination of the two).

Common shortcomings

Must bars always be aligned at one end?

Aligned bars allow a more accurate comparison, revealing even small differences in the data set. Bars or other length representations, however, are sometimes effective even when not aligned. Examples are divided bars (showing fractions), bars representing positive and negative values as lengths in opposite directions from the axis, and intervals shown in a position representation, as for confidence intervals around data points.

How can I compare a large number of data?

Both the bar and the dot charts remain useful up to medium-size data sets. Like most graphs, they can be drawn small and remain readable. With the data ordered from largest to smallest, they ensure that the closest values in the data (the ones most difficult to tell apart visually) are next to each other, for an easier comparison.

A large bar or dot chart, however, is much like a long list: it is structured as a chain, not a tree. Hence it can usefully be divided, for example with a little extra spacing, into groups of data, providing a simple instance of visual hierarchy. As in a table, these groups are ideally logical, but, if not, they can simply group data by five, to make for an easier visual correspondence between labels and corresponding bars or dots.

I was told that pie charts should never be used. Do you concur?

Pie charts are a good choice for a lay audience, perhaps, but they certainly lack the accuracy of alternative representations. They are also hard to align with the other items on the page.

Vertical bars (columns) do not accommodate labels as well as horizontal ones. Labels set vertically are hard to read; horizontal ones spread out the bars so much that their comparison becomes difficult.

Dot charts, being position representations, should unmistakably be recognized as such. To this end, guiding lines should extend over the whole width. If they stop at the data point instead, they suggest a length much more than a position representation.

Bar charts, being based on a length representation, do not accommodate whiskers ("error bars") well. The one-sided whisker ingrained in the life sciences is hardly intuitive, as it requires a projection effort. To use whiskers, prefer a position representation.

Comparing data

Population [millions]

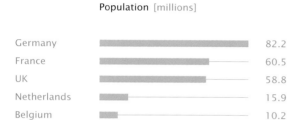

Germany		82.2
France		60.5
UK		58.8
Netherlands		15.9
Belgium		10.2

Life expectancy at birth [years]

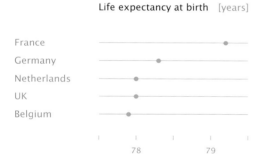

France	
Germany	
Netherlands	
UK	
Belgium	

78　　79

A STRAIGHTFORWARD WAY to compare numerical data is to represent them by lines or bars of proportional length, aligned at one end. To respect the proportion among the data, bars must of course be shown in full (from zero): partial bars are misleading, even when accompanied by an explicit scale. Bars are best drawn horizontally, so they can be labeled easily or be combined with a table, in which case they need no scale. They can usefully be ordered from largest to smallest length, unless the data set suggests another, more meaningful order.

Close data values, poorly resolved by a length representation, are best encoded as positions along a scale, marked by dots: indeed, this scale need not run from zero to be meaningful, so it can spread data apart, for a more accurate comparison. Such "dot charts" also accommodate additional information more easily than bar charts do; they can thus show subsets or add confidence intervals with whiskers around data points. They too can usefully order the data from largest to smallest.

Pie charts, a common way to represent fractions, are intuitive but are not very accurate: they fail to reveal small differences. They are best replaced by bar or dot charts, which combine nicely with a small table (perhaps one showing both relative and absolute values), can display negative values if needed, and fit better in sharply defined page layouts. Multiple pies that must be compared can also be replaced by divided bars.

Black Eagle Holding　　Net profit in 2008

Asset mgmt
10%

Insurance
24%

Retail banking
32%

Merchant
banking
34%

Black Eagle Holding　　Net profit in 2008

Merchant banking	34%		245
Retail banking	32%		230
Insurance	24%		173
Asset management	10%		72
			$ 720 million

Summarizing data sets

Should the axis be horizontal or vertical?

The optimal orientation of the axis depends on the need for labeling and for comparison with adjacent displays, and on the page layout. Individual data points are more clearly labeled when placed along a vertical axis. By contrast, (sub)sets are easier to label when horizontal.

When showing all data, how can one show data points having exactly the same value?

Data points that have exactly the same value or values so close that they coalesce visually can be set apart in the direction perpendicular to the axis (producing, in a sense, a histogram).

What are whiskers best used for?

Whiskers should show a meaningful interval, in view of the message or research question. When you merely want to display distribution, use whiskers to show percentiles in a box plot. To allow a statistical inference about the mean of the larger population of which the data set is a random sample, use whiskers to indicate a confidence interval around the sample mean (not the standard deviation or standard error of the mean). In any case, indicate what you use.

A visual summary of a given data set is often useful, especially toward comparison with other data sets. Summaries, of course, fail to provide a full picture of the distribution of the data and should therefore be used carefully and for large enough data sets.

The combination of mean and standard deviation (a two-point summary) affords but a limited view of a distribution, especially one that is non-Gaussian. The mean is sensitive to the presence of outliers, and a single indication of variability is insufficient to reveal an asymmetrical or complex distribution. As an illustration of these two severe limitations, the four distributions below, visibly very different, have the same mean and same standard deviation. Box plots provide more discriminating summaries, though showing the full data set, perhaps together with the mean or median, may be the best option.

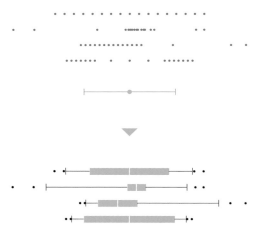

Summarizing a small data set makes little sense. A box plot for a set of six data uses seven values (five percentiles and two outliers)—in other words, one *more* value than data in the set—and only two of these are actual data rather than interpolations. For such small data sets, display all individual data.

Displaying distribution

THE DISTRIBUTION OF THE DATA in a univariate data set often provides a useful overview of this set—one that can, if needed, be compared to that of other data sets (or subsets), whether in a detailed view or in the form of a visual summary.

Showing the entire data set as points positioned along a scale is probably the most accurate way to convey its distribution. The resulting display is simple, univariate like the data set, and truthful to individual data. It can easily identify subsets with different markers or at different distances from the axis. For large data sets, however, it quickly becomes impractical.

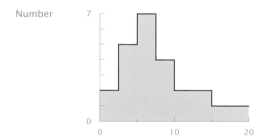

Histograms reduce the data set somewhat by grouping data in equivalent intervals, positioned along the horizontal scale, and showing as a vertical length the number of individual data in each interval, as absolute value or as percentage of the total (to compare histograms showing data sets of different sizes). While fairly intuitive to interpret, they can be very sensitive to the origin and the width of the intervals used to group data: a different choice of intervals (wider, narrower, or just offset) may result in a very different picture of the data distribution. Because they use a length representation, their vertical scale must run from zero. For an easy interpretation of the fraction of total data in a large interval, the vertical bars must touch: the fraction is then read as the (relative) area under the curve.

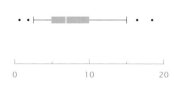

Box plots and related representations summarize the data set down to a few points. Traditional Tukey boxes, with whiskers and a central point, are five-point summaries, corresponding to the 10th, 25th, 50th (median), 75th, and 90th percentiles, but they can easily be extended to be nine-point summaries and can be complemented by individual extremes or outliers. Summaries are limiting, especially for complex distributions, such as multimode ones, so they must be used with caution. Still, they allow an easy comparison between subsets of data, each summarized by one box, all placed along the same scale.

For three continuous variables, how about a two-dimensional scatter plot, with circles of varying size to encode the third variable?

Encoding a third variable as the size of a circle used as the data marker raises several issues. The audience may not be sure whether to look at the radius or at the area of the circles shown, and the perceived proportion is neither of these anyway. Also, the three variables do not receive equal treatment—a possible further distortion.

How about a multiple-bar chart to compare two variables on a point-by-point basis?

Even when the aim is not to reveal correlation, a scatter plot typically provides more insight into the data set, by offering a better overview than a multiple-bar chart. A diagonal line helps compare the values of the respective variables.

An alternative option is to draw two dot charts (one for each variable) and to connect the dots across the charts. Such displays are typically used for evolutions, as when the two variables are really one variable at two different times, in which case the slope of the connecting line is a meaningful representation of the variation. Still, they cannot accommodate as many data as scatter plots: they rapidly become cluttered.

Although bar charts afford an intuitive comparison of univariate data, they do not work nearly as well when trying to show two or more variables at once. The multiple bars or divided bars used in this case hinder comparison and fail to display distribution.

A scatter plot is a more effective tool for exploring bivariate data: by mapping out their distribution, it readily reveals relations and points out outliers.

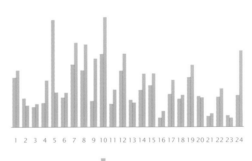

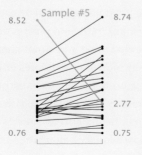

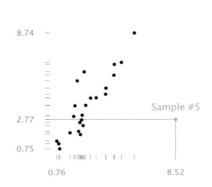

Revealing correlations

Unemployment rate [%]

Spain
Greece
Italy
France
Finland
European Union
Belgium
Germany
Denmark   Sweden
Portugal   United Kingdom
Austria
Netherlands   Ireland
Lux.

Females

Males

SAT scores   Writing

Mathe-
matics

Critical
reading

CORRELATION BETWEEN two or more continuous variables, especially when the variables are not sequenced in time, is revealed clearly by a scatter plot. This direct extension of the dot chart is a simple, powerful, yet underused display.

By encoding the data as positions along two orthogonal scales, a two-dimensional scatter plot reveals the shape and strength of the relation between two variables, together with outliers. It can easily identify subsets with different markers, although these must be well contrasted, lest the display look cluttered. When the form of the relation between the variables is known, the scatter plot can show the corresponding regression curve. In small data sets, individual points can be labeled if relevant.

A scatter plot is an effective exploratory graph for data sets of two continuous variables, even if no correlation is sought. By spreading the data in two orthogonal directions, it reveals their distribution along the two variables, mapping them out. Projecting the points onto the axes would show the marginal, univariate distributions for each of the continuous variables.

Three-dimensional scatter plots, representing three variables as positions along three orthogonal scales in perspective view, are direct generalizations of the two-dimensional scatter plot but are often more difficult to visualize, hence less insightful. A better alternative for three (or more) continuous variables is a matrix juxtaposition of two-dimensional scatter plots— one for each pair of variables—not unlike a chart of distances between cities: the relation between two variables is plotted in a panel at the intersection of the matching row and column. Because panels focus on visualizing the shape and strength of correlations between a possibly large number of variables, they are drawn small and sober, typically without any scale. Nonetheless, data points of special interest, such as outliers, can usefully be labeled or even connected across the panels. Relevant panels may be repeated separately, then with scales.

Does a line plot make sense for variables that do not vary continuously over time, for example a monthly financial result?

The line in a line plot can be regarded either as representing the continuous variable itself, perhaps as an interpolation between the data, or as merely connecting the set of data points. A variable taking one value per time interval can meaningfully be shown to evolve over time (that is, from one interval to the next), as long as it is clear that the only meaningful data are the dots—and not the line connecting the dots. The slope of each line segment is meaningful, though: it reveals the change per unit of time.

In simple cases, the very nature of the variable indicates whether a line is a meaningful interpolation. For example, an uninterrupted series of yearly values would be readily understood as connected, but not interpolated, by the line. A missing yearly value in the series, however, would create ambiguity, unless the data points are explicitly identified as such, with markers.

How about showing two dependent variables expressed in different units in the same panel, with one scale left and another scale right?

Data lines in the same panel are unavoidably compared, but this comparison is meaningless if the variables are expressed in different units. By changing the two scales, we can for example make the lines intersect anywhere, each time leaving the viewers with a very different picture.

To draw variables expressed in different units along one scale, show their relative evolution: divide each of them by some reference value (in the same units) to get a dimensionless ratio.

Bar charts, effective for comparing univariate data, are a suboptimal display for multivariate data sets. If the bar labels are values of a continuous variable, position them correctly along an appropriate scale: equidistant bars for what are nonequidistant data will suggest an erroneous correlation or evolution.

Even if you see each data point as a different case, consider connecting the dots to show an evolution, so the slope of the connecting line reveals variation. Switching from bars to lines is all the more needed for multiple dependent variables. A multiline plot allows a comparison not only among adjacent data but also among evolutions of the different variables.

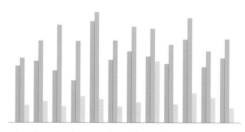

Showing evolution

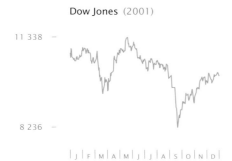

Dow Jones (2001)

11 338 –

8 236 –

| J | F | M | A | M | J | J | A | S | O | N | D |

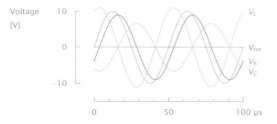

Voltage [V]

10

0

−10

V_L
V_{tot}
V_R
V_C

0   50   100 µs

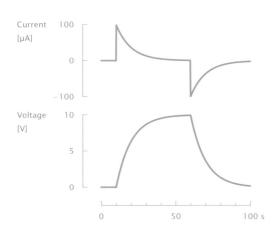

Current [µA]

100

0

−100

Voltage [V]

10

5

0

0   50   100 s

W HEN ONE OF THE VARIABLES can be seen as monotonic, the corresponding sequence can be shown as a line plot. This "scatter plot with connected dots" reveals the evolution of a so-called dependent variable versus the monotonic one, also called independent variable. This variable, typically time, runs best along a horizontal scale, increasing from left to right, with the dependent variable running along the vertical scale.

A line plot turns out to be appropriate for both experimental and calculated data. In all cases, it must show the data points unambiguously. When adjacent data points are close enough, notably in calculated data where they can be arbitrarily close, they need not be shown individually: a line typically suffices. Otherwise, they are best shown as "dots connected by a line," because a line alone might misrepresent the limited data set.

Line plots can readily display the evolution of two (or more) dependent variables versus the same independent variable. If all the dependent variables are expressed in the same units, they can be displayed along the same scale in a single panel. If not, they must be displayed in distinct, juxtaposed panels, with different vertical scales and a common horizontal one.

When the evolution of a dependent variable must be displayed against two independent ones, the line plot can be extended to three dimensions, as a surface often represented by a mesh. Three-dimensional plots drawn in perspective view, however, are hard to visualize, more so for some people than for others, and should be used with caution. They can suggest the shape of the surface but make individual data points hard to read off the axes. Moreover, they are sensitive to the viewing angle, as part of the surface may be masked. Depending on the data, alternative displays in two dimensions are cross sections (plot of dependent variable versus first independent variable, repeated for different values of second independent variable) or possibly contour lines, like those on a topographical map.

Can a display become too complex?

Just like any other communication component, a display can be too complex for its audience or in view of the constraints of space and time. Still, what makes displays too complicated is most often a suboptimal spatial arrangement of its panels. To keep the perception global, align the panels visually in meaningful groups of up to five—both horizontally and vertically.

What is the optimal size for a graph?

Finding the most appropriate size for a graph is not automatic: one must take into account not only the data displayed but also the page or slide on which the graph must be inserted, to achieve an effective and harmonious whole.

Graphs in reports and on slides are often drawn unnecessarily large for the data set they display, wasting space that could be put to better use, such as having text next to the graph in a report or larger margins around the graph on a slide. As a rough guide, question the size of graphs that take up more space than you would need for a table listing the same data as in the graph.

At the other end of the spectrum, small graphs are seldom too small for the data they display but may no longer accommodate legible labels or distinguishable data markers, in particular on devices that suffer from limited resolution, such as projected computer screens. Limiting text labels, numbers, and data markers can help.

Beyond the size of the graph in itself, optimize such parameters as font size and line thickness, especially if you scale the display up or down. Many slides have huge graphs... with a tiny font.

Constructing complex displays

Complex data sets (those including many variables) may require complex displays, with enough panels to search for correlations or compare evolutions among continuous variables, or to display subsets resulting from the presence of discrete variables. These panels must then be meaningfully organized on the page, to show the structure of the data set: panels with a common horizontal or vertical scale are thus best placed under or beside one another, respectively (with the scale appearing only once), panels showing subsets must use the same scales, etc. Principles of proximity, similarity, prominence, and sequence apply here as they do for page layout: the display must indeed provide insight as a whole.

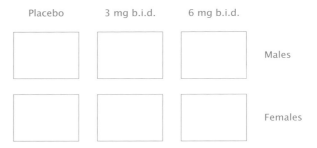

In contrast, data sets including but few variables seldom require complex—or even large—displays, even when they include many values per variable. Effective graphical displays can convey many data in a small space and can often be reduced in size without loss of clarity as long as labels are legible. Small graphs are particularly appropriate as panels in complex displays, where their size allows richer, clearer spatial arrangements. Such small multiples are usually clearest with as few labels as possible. They can often do without the scales, for example.

The sample histograms at right take up less than 0.5 cm^2 each (and could be drawn smaller still), yet they still allow comparisons.

Comparing groups of data

Single panel, multiple lines

Multiple panels

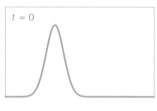

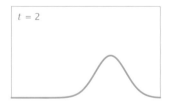

ISCRETE VARIABLES, dividing the data set into subsets, can be represented in either of two fundamental ways: the subsets can be shown in a single panel and distinguished by a visual difference such as marker shape or line thickness, or they can be shown in as many separate, juxtaposed panels. A single panel allows a more accurate comparison of subsets but may not provide a satisfactory view of individual subsets when data points are numerous and subsets largely overlap.

When the data set involves more than one discrete variable, the resulting displays can use multiple devices, for example different marker shapes, each in solid and hollow versions, or multiple panels organized both horizontally and vertically. They can of course use a combination of the two approaches.

Multiple panels representing subsets of the same variables must use the same scales to offer a meaningful comparison. By contrast, multiple panels representing different variables, as in a matrix plot, may use a different scale for each variable, for example in an effort to resolve closely grouped data better.

Life expectancy	Males	Females
France		
Germany		
Netherlands		
UK		
Belgium		

74   75   76   80   81   82   83

	Population [millions]		Density [inhab./km²]	
Germany		82.2		236
France		60.5		90
UK		58.8		245
Netherlands		15.9		468
Belgium		10.2		358

Constructing the graph

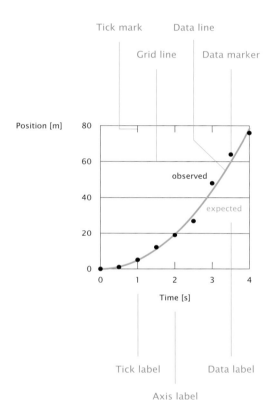

Tick mark   Data line

Grid line   Data marker

Position [m]   80

observed

expected

Time [s]

Tick label   Data label

Axis label

OOR CONSTRUCTION RUINS otherwise effective graphs by accidentally distorting the data, making them hard to read out, or distracting the viewers with decoration. When constructing your graphs, too, adapt to your audience, maximize the signal-to-noise ratio, use effective redundancy.

Dimension the graphs according to the size and the nature of the data set, in harmony with the rest of the page. Graphs need not be large to reveal the data or to convey a message: small graphs often work well. Unless the data or page layout suggest otherwise, make the graphs wider than they are tall; to show evolution, run the independent variable horizontally. Select ranges that are intuitive for the audience and the data, that spread the data over the panel, and, in complex displays, that allow undistorted comparisons among the various panels. When using a length representation, run the range from zero.

Quiet the background. Question the need for axes, especially when grid lines are present or when the data reveal the scale. Set the axis labels horizontally, including for the vertical axis. Question the use of grid lines, which allow a detailed readout but are seldom needed to convey a message. Limit the number of tick marks and labels: divide ranges in two to five intervals and, if useful, each interval further in two or five subintervals. Regardless of the range, label tick marks with intuitive values, normally in a progression of 1, 2, or 5×10^n. To reveal the data, replace the conventional, equidistant grid lines, tick marks, and corresponding labels by data-relevant ones that indicate, for example, the range of data or some data points of interest.

Make the data stand out against the (low-noise) background. As a rule, prefer simple, solid data markers (circles, by default); use hollow markers for contrast with nearby solid ones only. Adjust the marker size to the number of markers and the size of the graph. Make data lines thicker than background lines. For an intuitive graph, use direct labels, not a separate legend.

When should I use a logarithmic scale?

Use a logarithmic scale to explore a relation that you suspect is logarithmic or exponential, or to compare change rates among variables having different units. Do not use this scale merely to redistribute largely different values. (Because a logarithmic scale does not include zero, do not use it with a length representation. Reserve it strictly for position representations.)

Should I place tick marks inside or outside the graphing area?

Tick marks unavoidably interfere somewhat with the data when inside the graphing area and with the rest of the page when outside of it. Prefer what interferes least for a single graph and what is consistent across all your graphs in a document. If necessary, adjust the range to reduce the interference between tick marks and data (unless this range starts from zero).

How should I distinguish data subsets?

In a display in which data subsets are visually separated (for example, lines that do not cross), a label next to each subset suffices to tell them apart. Otherwise, use distinct markers (circle, square, etc.) or distinct lines (solid, dashed, etc.), in addition to the labels identifying the subsets.

Well-chosen colors help distinguish subsets, too, but not everyone distinguishes all colors well, and projected colors may not look as intended. Therefore, when using color, use it redundantly. As a test, convert your display to gray levels, as when printing it on a black-and-white printer, and verify that you can still identify everything.

In a graphical display, the "signal" is the data set. In first approximation, any nondata item is noise. So is, of course, a needlessly redundant encoding of the data, for example a third dimension on bars. (As a rule, use no more dimensions in your graph than continuous variables in the data set it shows, and beware of three-dimensional representations anyway, as these distort the perception of the data.)

Beyond the usual, purely decorative paraphernalia (perspective effects, color gradients, and the like), perhaps the most common noise source in graphs is inappropriate scales, especially those generated automatically by graphing applications. Any scale is fully defined with just two tick marks; therefore one needs a positive reason to put more than two. Helping the viewer read out the values of the data is the usual reason, but it deserves careful thought. What numbers will the viewer likely want to know? Can we provide these exact numbers on the scale instead of obliging the viewer to interpolate them? In any case, the scales drawn should be intuitive and uncluttered: a scale sporting more tick marks than the number of data simply makes no sense.

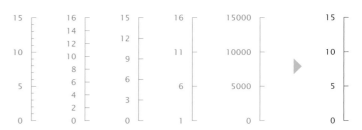

After reducing or eliminating the noise in a display, consider increasing the signal by making the data more prominent: use simple, solid data markers (a circle, by default) and thick enough data lines. These usually allow just as accurate comparisons.

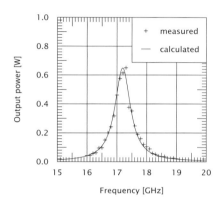

A poor graph

The graph exhibits a very low signal-to-noise ratio, with excessive tick marks and uncalled-for grid lines, and comparatively little ink to represent the data.

The graph is not intuitive, for the separate legend (a key to the symbols) prevents global processing. In a sense, it is a graph to *read*, not a graph to *view*.

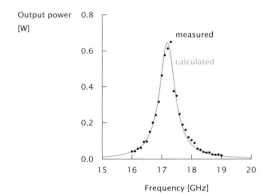

A good graph

The graph is plainer and therefore better contrasted: the background no longer interferes with the data, yet it provides sufficient information about them.

The graph is more intuitive: the labels, positioned next to the data, provide the required clarification where it is needed (when viewers look at the data).

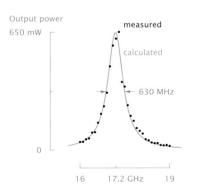

A better graph

The graph shows the data and nothing but the data: tick marks are relevant, not arbitrarily equidistant; nondata lines are gray, to make the data prominent.

The graph readily answers questions about the peak (position, height, and full width at half maximum) and about the range over which data were acquired.

Drafting the caption

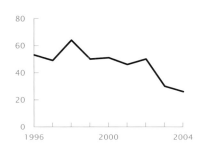

Evolution of the sales of Colayol
as a function of time (1996-2002).

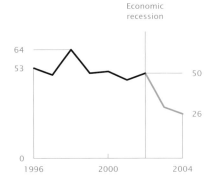

The Colayol sales have dropped
by 50% over the last two years,
following the recession in 2002.

LIKE CHILDREN, adults browsing a document are typically more attracted to any pictures in it than to the text. The figures of a document, together with their caption, are thus a first and great opportunity to get messages across. For maximum impact, figures are best reserved for messages, that is, for interpreting information, not merely for storing it. Data storage is best entrusted to tables, located in an appendix.

Pictures without words, however, are intrinsically ambiguous. As much as they might try to emphasize some aspect visually, they may still suggest different meanings to different viewers and often suggest very little unless clarified by an explanation. Thus they leave readers with either or both of these questions: *what am I looking at?* and *why are you showing this to me?* The first can be answered with a title and perhaps clear labels, as for the axes of a graph; the second calls for a verbal message.

What to call the added verbal message is a matter of definition. Although *caption* generally designates whatever words or text accompany a table or graphical display, it restrictively refers to a descriptive title, not a grammatically complete sentence. In contrast, a *legend* is a comment or explanation, consisting of one or more complete sentences. (To add to the confusion, *legend* also designates a key—an explanatory list of symbols.) A caption states what the table or figure is (the *what*) whereas a legend explains, perhaps among other things, what the table or figure illustrates (the *so what*, that is, the intended message).

To convey a message effectively to the audience, figures thus need a legend more than a caption. They might provide both (first a caption, then a legend, run together as one paragraph), but a well-phrased *so what* makes a separate *what* redundant. The legend must be explicit enough for the figure and legend to make sense separately from the main text, as when readers are browsing the document, yet it is best kept short, to avoid hindering the otherwise fast processing of the visual codings.

Example is the school of mankind,
and they will learn at no other.

— Edmund Burke

An expert is a man who has made
all the mistakes which can be made…

— Niels Bohr

Applications

THE PRINCIPLES discussed in the previous four parts have broad applicability. Any document, for example, can usefully state upfront what readers want to know first of all and most of all, in the form of a global component. Still, selecting what to include in this component may prove less straightforward for some document types than for others. More generally, the universal underlying ideas might need to be particularized according to the document's objective.

This final part sketches out more specific recommendations for five common types of document. First, it discusses how to plan, design, draft, format, and revise sets of instructions. Moving from traditional paper documents to electronic ones, it offers guidelines for writing and managing electronic mail and for revealing the structure and facilitating the navigation of Web sites. Next, it considers meeting reports and, finally, a type of document more akin to slides: the scientific poster.

Effective instructions

USER MANUALS or more generally sets of instructions are among the most challenging documents to write. Users read instructions, not to learn about features, but to perform tasks. More than any other type of document, instructions must therefore be user-centric and task-oriented: they must allow the users to locate the information they need and provide this information in a way that helps them perform all the required actions and nothing but the required actions.

The purpose and audience for instructions are often multiple. This multiplicity warrants modular documents, with a part for each purpose or audience. One part might thus indicate what the product does, as with a reference manual; another might explain how to perform specific tasks, as in a tutorial or a set of instructions; and yet a third might help the users diagnose and correct problems, as in a troubleshooting guide.

Like any other document or section thereof, manuals or sets of instructions can usefully start with a global component, to orient the users about both the product and the document. This component should let them know what the instructions are about and help them locate what they need to get started, in terms not only of process (where to start in the document) but also of equipment (what is provided with the product and what else they need to complete the tasks). In particular, the object of the document or section should help each user decide what part of the document to read for what purpose.

Identifying yourself as user

Why/when	To access your personal profile or to carry out your transactions,
What	you must first log in to the system using your ID card together with the user name and password you received as part of your contract.
How	To log in, proceed in three steps: …

For each task, help users make decisions about what to do. Before the actual instructions, state the objectives: indicate what the task does and why or when they would want to do it. Along the way, reassure them as to their progress in the task. After the task, provide elements for navigation: remind them of what they have just completed and where they can go next. To help them identify tasks, write action-oriented headings (*Identifying yourself as user*, as opposed to *User identification*).

Common shortcomings

What is wrong with the passive voice?

As the name fittingly states, the passive voice is less conducive to action and, in particular, less focused on the user than the imperative. By expressing a need or obligation, it suggests the appropriate action implicitly at best, so it is far less straightforward. A sentence such as *ID badges must be worn visibly at all times* is more likely to result in intellectual agreement (*Indeed they must*) than in actual commitment. In contrast, sentences in the imperative mood such as *Wear your ID badge visibly at all times* leave no doubt as to whom the action concerns.

Is the imperative mood not too direct?

Usually, the imperative mood is appropriately direct, at least for instruction sets in English. Feel free to use the word *please* in front of it when your instruction is really a request, as in *Please fill out the attached form and return it ….*

Other languages, and their associated cultures, might be less tolerant of the imperative mood and might moreover require a delicate choice between familiar and formal second persons. In this case, an infinitive verb may be an option: it retains the strength of an active verb form while appearing to be less directive to the user.

How many screen shots should I include?

How often you should include an illustration depends on many factors, from the audience and its familiarity with the product or process possibly all the way to the production budget. Tests with representative users can help you decide what instructions should be illustrated.

An action stated implicitly as a need or obligation often fails to make readers feel concerned about it. Instead of a passive voice, use an imperative mood.

Victims of a chemical spill need to be placed under the shower at once.

If a coworker is affected by a chemical spill, place him or her under the shower at once.

A condition stated after the action might be read too late, that is, after the action has been performed. Place conditions (and warnings) before the action.

Click *OK*, unless you would like to modify the default values for the execution, in which case you should click *Options*.

If you would like to modify the default values for the execution, click *Options*. Otherwise, click *OK*.

A description of what the product can or cannot do fails to tell users what they can or should do with it.

The Gaap application will not work without a hardware key plugged into a USB port.

To use the Gaap application, first plug the hardware key in a free USB port. If you do not have a hardware key, …

1	Insert your ID card in the reader
2	The screen displays "User name?"
3	Key in your eight-digit user name
4	The screen displays "Password?"
5	Key in your four-digit password
6	The screen displays "Welcome…"
7	Should you get "Login error", pull out your ID card and start again

1 **Insert your ID card in the reader**
The screen displays "User name?"

2 **Key in your eight-digit user name**
The screen displays "Password?"

3 **Key in your four-digit password**
The screen displays "Welcome…"

Should the screen display "Login error", pull out your ID card and start again.

At every level in the instructions, let the users know not only what to do and why, but also how to do it and in what order. Prepare the users for the different steps they must carry out by providing an overview of the task or, if needed, subtasks. Be chronological: place decisions or warnings before actions, that is, use an *if … then do …* construction, not a *do … if …* one. Help the users check the success of their actions: tell them what to notice in response to the action they just carried out. As much as possible, tell users what corrective action to take, should they get a different response than the one announced.

Focus your drafting on what the readers must do. Separate these actions from other material such as system responses, comments, or warnings; for example, if you number the steps, do not number the items that are not actions to be carried out. Organize the actions into a balanced, consistent tree structure: although steps are obviously part of a sequence, group them into a hierarchical set of tasks and subtasks to avoid a chain. Describe similar steps with similar language, both in semantics and in syntax. In particular, express an action as a command (*Insert the card …*), not as a need (*The card must be inserted …*); in other words, use the imperative mood, not the passive voice.

Format the instructions to reveal their hierarchical structure and to differentiate actions from other material. Use pictures both to clarify required actions and to show product response. To avoid irrelevant details in pictures, prefer line drawings to photographs or, for software, partial screens to full ones.

More than other documents, instructions benefit from a test. Ensure that this test is realistic: place representative users in representative conditions. Observe what these users do, in what order they do it, and how they use the instructions. In other words, consider both the end result and the process. As always when testing documents, be ready to make changes: if anything goes wrong, blame the instructions, not the users.

Fundamentals

The name of the game
The three laws of communication
A thousand words, a thousand pictures
Chains and magical numbers
Trees, maps, and theorems

Effective written documents

Planning the document
Designing the document
Drafting the document
Formatting the document
Revising the document

Effective oral presentations

Planning the presentation
Designing the presentation
Creating slides
Delivering the presentation
Answering questions

Effective graphical displays

Understanding pictures
Planning the graph
Designing the graph
Constructing the graph
Drafting the caption

Applications

Effective instructions
Effective electronic mail
Effective Web sites
Effective meeting reports
Effective scientific posters

Effective electronic mail

ELECTRONIC MAIL (e-mail) has invaded our professional and personal lives, for better or worse. Well managed, it is faster, less formal, and more economical than post, yet less disruptive and more manageable than phone calls. Poorly used, however, it is an impediment more than a help, burying valuable information in endless, unstructured chains of hasty messages. For more effective e-mail communication, apply the same care to e-mail as you do to other documents.

Address e-mail to whoever must take action; put in *cc* whoever must be informed (but not act). Express the subject in two parts: a global topic and a specific one.

Do quote whatever original text provides context for your reply, but edit out unnecessary parts.

As a rule, open with a salutation: it is helpful to people in *cc*, too.

State agents, actions, and dates accurately (*who does what when*). Strive to be clear and concise, too, as always in written documents.

If the addressee must take action, indicate so politely, yet explicitly.

Close in a way that is appropriate to the e-mail's content and tone.

Identify yourself in more detail (yet concisely) whenever useful.

From	Jay Hell ‹jay@devilsworks.com›
Date	Fri 22 Feb 2008 14:17:45 +0100
To	Carolina Panounou ‹editor@folles.org›
CC	Gini Contabile ‹treasurer@folles.org›
Subject	**March Newsletter: article by Monday**

> Can you draft an article … for the March Newsletter?

Carolina,

I can draft the requested article tomorrow (Saturday), but I would like Gini to review it before I pass it on to you. Assuming she can take care of this on Sunday, I would have the final article ready for you by Monday.

Is Monday still in time for the March Newsletter? Please let me know.

Best regards,
-- Jay

CEO, Devil's Works
www.devilsworks.com

Receiving less e-mail

Should I reply to every message?

If the message is addressed primarily to you (your name appears under *to*), then you should probably reply, even if only to acknowledge it. If you are in *cc*, you are not expected to reply, which does not mean that you are not allowed to react, should you consider it useful to do so.

Why should I acknowledge e-mail messages?

E-mail delivery on networks such as the Internet can be regarded as a best-effort service only. There is thus no guarantee that the addressee has received, let alone read, a given message: messages can be deleted without notification by filters or even accidentally by the recipient, be delivered to an out-of-service mailbox, etc.

In the absence of a reply, senders may worry that their message has not been received, yet be unsure about sending a verification e-mail. If a message you receive requires no answer, you may nonetheless want to tell the sender that you understand it or that you agree with it. Similarly, if you are not going to respond soon (that is, not as fast as the sender would expect), you can reassure him or her that you received the e-mail and will respond to it by a given date.

When should I use attachments?

Use attachments for material that recipients are likely to work with (modify, print, or file). Place in the e-mail message itself any content that they will likely read immediately on screen. Ensure each of the two can be read on its own. Consider the need for redundancy, too: often, the e-mail can be an abstract of the attachment.

If you are buried under too much incoming e-mail, you may feel helpless about it. Yet, without hoping for a revolution, you can still take concrete steps toward easing the overload. To receive less e-mail, simply send less e-mail—and send better e-mail, too.

Many e-mails are sent in response to other e-mails. By sending fewer messages, you will likely receive fewer replies or follow-ups, too. Also, if everyone sends less e-mail, everyone will receive less as well, at least on average. This is not to say, of course, that you should stop communicating with others as expected of you: do send what you have to send. For the same total information, however, you can often send fewer messages by thinking carefully through the issue before hitting the send button. Perhaps you can send these to fewer people, too, such as by using distribution lists with due restraint.

Carefully drafted e-mail is also more likely to elicit the desired response—no more, no less—thereby reducing the need for reminder messages or the risk of a piecemeal answer across multiple messages. Be explicit about what you request; if you require several answers, consider itemizing your questions. Instead of an endless, reverse-chronological chain of previous exchanges at the end of your message, provide some useful context at the beginning of it, to bring your readers more effectively to the point.

Much sloppiness in e-mail stems from the fast pace of the exchanges, making these no more than chat. To decrease the quantity and increase the quality of e-mail, try slowing it down by introducing delays. Instead of replying immediately and perhaps hastily to e-mail (thus often triggering more exchanges), reply later—for example, the next day. In this way, you are more likely to provide a thoughtful reply, and, because of the delay, the addressee is likely to read your reply more carefully, too. E-mail thus regains the advantages of written communication.

How to effectively manage professional e-mail depends much on the requirements of your work. Here are general guidelines.

Read incoming e-mail three times or more on a working day, including when you arrive and a little before you plan to leave. Decide what to do about each incoming message immediately after reading it, even if you carry out the decided action later.

Reply to e-mail within a few working days (on the same day for urgent messages, within a week for the less urgent ones). If you anticipate replying later than the sender might expect, let him or her know in advance by when he or she will receive your reply. If you plan to be away from your e-mail for more than one day, consider setting up an out-of-office autoreply.

Address e-mail only to those who must act (decide, reply, etc.), with a copy to those who must be informed (most often, solely of the outcome of the discussion, not of the ongoing details). Be selective: avoid addressing or copying people automatically, as with a reply to all or with a company-wide distribution list, or on a systematic "just in case" basis, as with your hierarchy.

Contextualize e-mail for all its recipients. In the subject line, state the global topic (typically the same for several messages), then a subtopic that is specific to the message. When replying, rewrite the subject line if it no longer describes the topic well. Quote the original message to situate your reply in its context, but keep the quotes short: replace unnecessary parts by "…."

Compose e-mail with just as much care as you would compose other professional documents, following the rules of grammar, spelling, punctuation, and propriety. In a plain-text medium, use a pair of *asterisks* or of _underscores_ in place of italics. Avoid all-uppercase text, viewed as the equivalent of shouting. Beware of humor, such as irony, which is difficult to recognize in a written text. If you do use some, indicate so, as with ";-)."

Effective Web sites

COMPARED TO A PRINTED DOCUMENT, a Web site has both advantages and drawbacks. Being interactive, it makes navigation easier, thanks to the hyperlinks. Going beyond static text and images, it becomes multimedia, adding sound or animation on demand. Because its structure and extent are harder to perceive than in a physical document, however, it can easily disorient visitors and make it difficult for them to assimilate the information in a structured way. To orient the visitors, make the site's structure conspicuous: give visitors a map, let them know where they are on the map, and tell them where they can go on (or in reference to) the map.

Make the corporate logo be a link to the corporate site's home page (now a widespread convention).

Make the navigational controls (the links) identifiable as such, and visually different from other controls (buttons, fields, etc.).

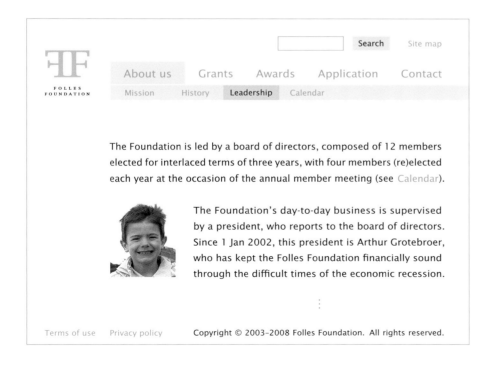

Display the top levels of the tree, indicating where the visitors are and where they can go (the links). Position all-encompassing items (search box, link to the site map) outside the site's main structure.

Position links outside sentences (perhaps as a parenthesis). Use the same words as on the map.

For legibility, avoid any patterned, textured, or picture background. Do not overlap text and pictures.

Position links to secondary items such as legal notices in a place easy to find, yet out of the way.

Common shortcomings

Why must visitors see the site's structure?
Is it not enough for them to find easily
the information they are looking for?

The need for structural clues depends in part
on the information-seeking task of the visitors.
When visitors are looking for a specific piece
of information, such as a telephone number,
they are usually content with having found it.
At the same time, they may be reassured to see
where they have found it, so they can evaluate
whether the piece is up-to-date or exhaustive.
When visitors are seeking general information,
however (that is, an open-ended task), they need
to know everywhere they can go and to be able
to recognize if they have been there previously,
if they are to complete their task methodically.

Should hyperlinks be underlined?

Underlined hyperlinks are a custom inherited
from early Web browsers. They made sense
on one-bit (black-and-white) screens, as one
of few highlighting possibilities, but are best
replaced today with more legible alternatives,
such as being set in a different color or style,
besides being recognizable by their location.

How should I clarify nonverbal hyperlinks?

Visual links, such as icons or clickable maps,
may be harder to identify as links than words.
As with all pictures, a companion explanation
in words is the surest way to lift the ambiguity,
not only to indicate that the picture is a link,
but also to clarify its destination or its action.
Displaying icons as a visually structured group
and locating them where visitors expect links
(such as at the top of the page) might help, too.

To navigate a site effectively, visitors must be able
to form a mental picture of how the various pages
fit together into a consistent, meaningful structure.
To this end, and besides a usually distinct site map,
a useful feature is showing the top-level structure
of the site as a group of hyperlinks at the top or side
of every page. This group of links must obviously
be consistent across pages: different pages offering
a different set of top-level links—even if these are
each time the most relevant ones—does not allow
visitors to figure out the main structure of the site.

A map can of course not orient visitors if it cannot
be brought in correspondence with the field reality.
Thus, pages not identified in reference to the map
(perhaps not identified at all in a recognizable way)
fail to let visitors determine where they are. Similarly,
pages (other than side explanations) not identified
on the site map make it difficult for their visitors
to go there again: the path must be remembered.
And links all pointing to the same destination, yet
phrased inconsistently or differently from the map,
make it hard for visitors to recognize the destination;
here, too, field and map do not seem to correspond.

Hyperlinks and other controls often fail to reveal
their action or to make it visible enough to visitors.
Some links are simply placed on the wrong words
(*To display a calendar, click here*): the link itself,
which normally stands out visually, gives no clue
as to its action, and links having different actions
are called the same (*click here*), which is suboptimal.
Hyperlinks grammatically embedded in a sentence
(*... as indicated on the calendar ...*) are less easily
recognizable as an action and cannot always use
the same wording as the map; moreover, visitors
will unlikely want to go elsewhere before finishing
to read the sentence. Finally, "mystery hyperlinks"
revealing their action only as the pointer passes
over them force visitors to uncover and remember
all actions before making their choice—a challenge.

About us   Grants   Awards   Application

Mission   History   **Leadership**   Calendar

About us > Leadership

... the annual member meeting (see Calendar).

A set of *start there* links

About us   Grants   Awards   Application

A *continue there* link

... the annual member meeting (see Calendar).

A *go there and back* link

... dropped over the last two years (display data).

Give visitors one or more maps. Show the site's main parts as a group of as many links, probably located on every page, perhaps with the substructure of the part currently visited. For complex sites, consider displaying the complete structure (the *site map*) on a distinct page, one that every page links to.

On each page, let the visitors know where they are on the map. If a (partial) map is displayed on the page, highlight the item corresponding to the part where they currently are. Otherwise, display a hierarchical, top-down path at the top of the page. In either case (map or path), every item can usefully be a link, except of course the item corresponding to the current page.

Tell visitors where they can go on (or in reference to) the map. Phrase links exactly as on the map: always use the same name for the same destination. Make links visible and identifiable as such, yet harmoniously integrated in the rest of the page: do not draw undue attention to them. Differentiate them from other items by their appearance, such as color or style, or their location on the page. To allow an easier navigation, group them in specific zones: at the top or bottom of the page, after a piece of text (in a zone labeled *Learn more about*), etc.

Navigational controls come in three categories, which might be dubbed *start there*, *continue there*, and *go there and back*. In the category *start there* are the links mapping out the site's structure, for example at the top of every page or in a site map, and devices allowing direct page access, such as a search box. A *continue there* link leads to another part of the page or site (a part identified as such on the site map) or to another site. Finally, a *go there and back* control points to side information, such as a definition, typically displayed in a different window.

Other controls must state their action clearly and consistently, to allow informed decisions. This action is best expressed as a verb phrase (*download file, clear form, submit request*, etc.).

Effective meeting reports

JUST LIKE OTHER WRITTEN DOCUMENTS, meeting reports benefit from a two-part structure: a global component, identifying the motivation for and outcome of the work (in this case, a meeting), followed by just enough details to justify this outcome or help readers understand it better. The report indeed need not be a detailed chronological record of everything said or done. A short account, perhaps stating the various viewpoints expressed, is often all that is needed to remind those who attended and inform those who did not (especially if they wanted to) of what happened at the meeting.

The header can usefully show not only the report's recipients (the usual *to* and *cc* lists) but also the meeting's members—both those who actually attended and those who could not. The lists of recipients and of members can often be combined, the members normally constituting the *to* list. Just as useful as each person's name is the reason why this person is taking part in the meeting or receiving the report, such as a function or membership in a working group involved in the meeting.

Who?	Members of the meeting and other recipients of the report
Why?	Motivation to hold a meeting (the same as in the invitation)
What?	Main outcome of the meeting: decisions, actions, and news
Details	What readers need to know to understand the outcome

The motivation must clarify who called the meeting and why. Structured like any foreword, it includes whatever context establishes the importance of the need, then states the need, the task (here, calling a meeting), and the object of the report, possibly including the agenda of the meeting. In other words, it is essentially the same as the invitation sent out to members.

The outcome of a meeting normally consists of decisions made, actions agreed upon, and perhaps "highlights"—that is, news or statements made at the meeting and worth stating upfront. These categories should be identified as such and should list items in a meaningful order—not necessarily chronologically. Action items, specifying who must do what by when, can thus be grouped either by owner or by topic, or listed by target date. They might even be attached in the form of a spreadsheet file or other format allowing them to be sorted in multiple ways.

Identifying people and actions

*How can I state a motivation
for a routine, periodic meeting?*

Even periodic meetings have a reason for being
if they are useful at all, and this reason can be
briefly recalled at the beginning of every report.
More useful still is clarifying the periodic nature
of the meeting, such as by stating its periodicity.
Numbering the meetings helps, too, especially
in case a planned meeting did not take place,
so nobody goes looking for what they think is
a missing report in the announced periodicity.

*How should I refer to attendees:
by first name, last name, initials?*

In the report's header, and for accuracy, refer
to attendees in full (first name and last name).
Elsewhere, use a system that is unambiguous
and carries the proper tone. You might simply
stick to what was used in meeting: for example,
if attendees called one another by first name,
it makes sense to use first names in the report,
too, possibly with the initial of the last name
if several attendees have the same first name.
In such a system, be sure to include first names
in the header, and use the full name to refer
to anyone outside the meeting. Consider also
whether first names might sound too informal
to secondary readers, such as those listed in *cc*.

Using initials or acronyms is common practice
in many organizations. While it is concise and,
if introduced well, unambiguous, this system
is less friendly to secondary readers, who may
not be familiar with the initials and will need
to look them up. Also, used within a sentence,
initials such as *JH* are somewhat less readable
than *Jay* or *Mr Hell* (consider what you would
say, if you were to read the sentence out loud).

Identifying people and actions in written reports
is all the more important when the topic discussed
involves managerial issues—as often in meetings:
management, indeed, is all about *who does what*
and *when* (and, to a lesser extent perhaps, *why*).
People and actions must thus be identified clearly
everywhere they come into play in meeting reports,
and more particularly so in the global component.

In the header, identify people by name and by role,
such as function in the organization, membership
in a committee, or simply responsibility in a project.
These roles, more than the people's names, help
the secondary readers understand in what capacity
each person was invited to take part in the meeting
or is sent a copy of the report. In the discussion,
you can refer to these people in one way or another
(by first name, by last name, or perhaps by initials)
without repeating their role, unless it is significant
for a given argument. Should you mention anyone
outside the meeting, mention his or her role, too.

In the list of actions decided upon, typically placed
on the first page as part of the global component,
indicate each time who must do what and by when.
As always, express the action in a verb, not a noun
(*provide a benchmark of* rather than *benchmark of*).
Use the plain form when the agent is not expressed
in the action itself; otherwise, conjugate the verb,
typically in the future tense (*Gini will provide a …*).
If you assign an action to several people, specify
which of them is accountable for its completion,
lest none of them take the initiative to carry it out.

Arrange the actions in whatever order is most useful
to your readers. You might group them by person,
so each attendee can easily retrieve all the actions
assigned to him or her. Within these groups, then,
you might order actions by priority or target date.
In contrast, grouping the actions by topic provides
readers in *cc* with a better overview of future work.

Indicate the periodicity of routine
meetings. Consider numbering
the reports, for a clear sequence.
Mention the date of the meeting,
as well as the start and end time.

List the members of the meeting,
that is, the people who attended
and those who normally should
have but did not (the *excused*).
Clarify who these members are
and why they are in the meeting.
(on the committee, as guest, etc.).

List the people not in the meeting
who receive a copy of the report.

State the reason for the meeting
and, if known, the date and time
(and the location) of the next one.

State who must do what by when.
Express each action with a verb.

Present actions in a useful order,
such as alphabetically by owner
(then, for each person, by date)
or grouped by topic—or perhaps
even presented in several ways.

Besides the actions agreed upon,
list upfront the decisions made,
if any, and perhaps the highlights.

FF

FOLLES
FOUNDATION

Quarterly fundraising meeting #12
Thu 20 Mar 2008, 10:00–11:30

Committee	Gini Contabile, *Treasurer*
	Carolina Panounou, *Newsletter editor*
	Nicolás Milia, *Vice-president* [excused]
Guest	Jay Hell, *CEO, Devil's Works*
Copy to	Arthur Grotebroer, *President*
	Monika Laklöter, *Secretary*

The Fundraising committee meets four times a year
to evaluate and decide on fundraising initiatives.
Next meeting: Mon 21 Jul 2008, 13:30–15:00

Owner	Action	Target date
Carolina	Ask Arthur to include fundraising in his next President's column	1 Apr 2008
	Inquire about the cost of running a half-page ad in local newspapers	20 Apr 2008
Gini	Provide a benchmark of fundraising for foundations such as ours (with Jay)	Next meeting

(Continue the list on additional pages, as needed.)

Effective scientific posters

An overcrowded, suitcase design
Items are squeezed where they fit, without any spatial coordination.

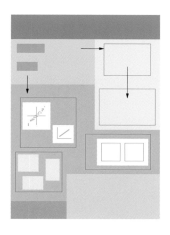

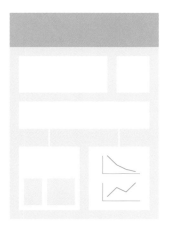

A large enough area for title, authors, etc.

A sequence of zones, sized as needed, yet spatially coordinated (white zones against a poster background, frame not necessary). Spatially coordinated, strongly visual items (photos, graphs, etc.) within the zones, too.

A clearer, more deliberate design
All items are coordinated in size and position into a logical pattern.

SCIENTIFIC POSTERS, summarizing a piece of research on one to two square meters of paper pinned on the wall, are best thought of as support for oral presentations, not as written documents. Viewers standing a meter away seldom feel like reading much text in this position, especially when authors are answering questions out loud next to them. Accordingly, posters can be designed like presentation slides, instead of presenting detailed evidence like scientific articles: they must convey messages, on their own (without requiring an oral explanation) and visually, with as little text as possible.

Compared to a set of slides, however, a poster is not divided automatically into a chronological succession of small frames. The design freedom thus afforded can usefully be harnessed to reveal the macrostructure of the research or of its account. In practice, alas, it is seldom used for more than trying to fit yet more information on the poster, by reshuffling elements like items in a suitcase—until one can squeeze the last one in. Authors often attempt to salvage such overcrowded designs with overly large headings, abundant frames and arrows, etc., thus making the posters even less inviting to passersby, be it at poster sessions or in the hallways of research laboratories.

One simple way to structure a poster visually is to think of it as a series of frames, after all—yet not necessarily the regular and somewhat restricting sequence offered by a set of slides, although printing A4 or US-letter sheets and arranging them in comic-strip fashion remains an option. While they may vary in size or aspect ratio, the different frames should be arranged into a clear, deliberate pattern: each of them should be placed where it makes sense, not (or not just) where there is space left. The intended processing sequence must be readily apparent, all the more so with frames in a matrix arrangement: must one look at them first down then across, or first across then down? The various "frames" need not be framed, really: they can be colored zones or, better, white zones on a colored background.

If I have seen further,
it is by standing on the shoulders of giants.

— Isaac Newton

Knowledge is of two kinds. We know a subject ourselves,
or we know where we can find information upon it.

— Samuel Johnson

Notes and references

18   The examples of premodifiers are from the menu of Cafe Pasqual's in Santa Fe, New Mexico (2001), and from *IEEE Trans. Ind. Appl.* 42:1, 21–30 (2006). This paper was pointed out to me by Thomas Vyncke.

55   The scientific abstract shown is a version rewritten with the help of Abigail Swillens of the abstract that appears in *J. Vasc. Surg.* 36, 598–604 (2002).

69   The example is from *Proc. ISSS'02*, 112–119 (2002).

73, 127   The four labels *proximity, similarity, prominence,* and *sequence* used to describe visual relationships were recommended to me by Karel van der Waarde.

98   The differential equation $\nabla \times \mathbf{B} = \mu_o \mathbf{J} + \mu_o \epsilon_o \partial \mathbf{E}/\partial t$ is Ampère's circuital law with Maxwell's correction (one of "Maxwell's equations" in electromagnetism).

125   The three labels *iconic, indexical,* and *symbolic* are from a well-known sign typology by Charles Peirce. Apple Records (left) is a division of Apple Corps Ltd. The Apple logo (right) is a trademark of Apple Inc. Eve accepting the apple is a detail from a painting by German Renaissance artist Albrecht Dürer (1507).

135, 139, 143   The population, life expectancy, and unemployment data for the year 2000 were obtained from Eurostat, the Statistical Office of the European Communities.

139   The SAT score averages of college-bound seniors by state in the USA for 2006–2007 were obtained from the National Center for Education Statistics.

141   The Dow Jones Industrial Index for the year 2001 (top) was obtained from Dow Jones & Company, Inc. The bottom two graphs illustrate time responses of a series RLC circuit and RC circuit, respectively.

149   The distinction between caption and legend is made in *The Chicago Manual of Style* (14th ed., 1993).

The principles and models discussed in this book have been shaped by my own professional practice, by all that I have read or heard on communication, and by the many rich discussions I have conducted with the participants in my training sessions. Most of these ideas have been around for quite a while (some of them for a few centuries or a few millennia), even if they may be expressed here in a new light, and few can in fact be attributed to a single person.

Early on, my thinking on effective communication was largely influenced by the various courses I took at Stanford University's Technical Communications Program with David Lougee and his team of tutors, and by the textbook used in one of these courses: *Technical Writing and Professional Communication for Nonnative Speakers of English* by Thomas Huckin and Leslie Olsen (second edition, McGraw-Hill, 1991).

Stanford is where I started teaching public speaking and developing my own ideas on what makes a talk effective. After attending a lecture by Gene Zelazny, I was convinced that slides should state a *so what*. In the following year, I formalized the *three laws of communication* that have proved so useful to me.

Around the same time, I was discovering the ideas of Edward Tufte as presented in *The Visual Display of Quantitative Information* (Graphics Press, 1983) and realizing that Tufte's "data-ink maximization" was in a sense maximizing the signal-to-noise ratio. I was also reading *The Elements of Graphing Data* by William Cleveland (Wadsworth, 1985) and thus learning about graphical perception and dot charts.

Except for those referenced on the opposite page, the example texts and graphs shown in this book were invented for the sole purpose of illustration. The names appearing in the examples are fictitious; any similarity to names of actual persons, products, or organizations is coincidental and unintentional.

Index of topics

Published in 2009 by Principiae
in Belgium (www.principiae.be)

Fifth printing, March 2020

ISBN 978 90 813677 07
D/2009/11.719/1

Photograph on back cover
by Joannes Vandermeulen